GH00793022

Praise for Arnol

'In Zable's sensitive hands, each individual story of survival belongs to all.' *Australian*

'No one writes about the immigrant experience in Australia quite like Arnold Zable…His books have an ethereal, myth-like quality, complete with beautifully lilting prose and near-tangible warmth.'
Big Issue

'Zable seeks to ennoble lives that might otherwise remain unheralded. His work recognises the basic decency of ordinary people and honours their struggles in the face of adversity.'
Age

'Arnold Zable is a writer who turns the unnoticed and the overlooked into something fine and lustrous.'
Courier-Mail

'The essential combined genius of Zable is that he can find a story of universal interest and tell it in such a way which commands universal attention.' *Australian Jewish News*

'Zable's vision is ultimately optimistic and affirming.'
Sydney Morning Herald

'Years of reflection and his own life experiences have contributed to the mastery with which Zable explores the themes of displacement, loss, nostalgia and homecoming in all of his books.' *Canberra Times*

'A master storyteller.' *Australian Book Review*

Also by Arnold Zable

Jewels and Ashes

Wanderers and Dreamers

Cafe Scheherazade

The Fig Tree

Scraps of Heaven

Sea of Many Returns

Violin Lessons

The Fighter

Arnold Zable is a highly acclaimed novelist, storyteller, educator and human rights advocate. He lives in Melbourne.
arnoldzable.com.au

The Watermill

Arnold Zable

TEXT PUBLISHING MELBOURNE AUSTRALIA

textpublishing.com.au

The Text Publishing Company
Swann House
22 William Street
Melbourne Victoria 3000
Australia

Copyright © Arnold Zable 2020

The moral right of Arnold Zable to be identified as the author of this work has been asserted.

All rights reserved. Without limiting the rights under copyright above, no part of this publication shall be reproduced, stored in or introduced into a retrieval system, or transmitted in any form or by any means (electronic, mechanical, photocopying, recording or otherwise), without the prior permission of both the copyright owner and the publisher of this book.

First published in Australia by The Text Publishing Company, 2020.

Cover design by Jessica Horrocks
Cover photo courtesy of the author
Page design by Text
Typeset by J&M Typesetters

Printed and bound in Australia by Griffin Press, part of Ovato, an accredited ISO/NZS 14001:2004 Environmental Management System printer.

ISBN: 9781922268556 (paperback)
ISBN: 978192923162 (ebook)

A catalogue record for this book is available from the National Library of Australia.

This book is printed on paper certified against the Forest Stewardship Council® Standards. Griffin Press holds FSC chain-of-custody certification SGS-COC-005088. FSC promotes environmentally responsible, socially beneficial and economically viable management of the world's forests.

To Aunty Joy Murphy Wandin, Wurundjeri elder
and to Zahra Shohani, 1994–2001

Improvement makes straight roads,
but the crooked roads without
improvement are roads of genius.

William Blake

The faintest ink is more powerful
than the strongest memory.

Chinese proverb

Contents

The Watermill *1*

The Ballad of Keo Narom *71*

Republic of the Stateless *115*

Where We Meet *205*

Author's Note *250*

The Watermill

I ask N to accompany me to the watermill as interpreter. The miller invites us inside and places the kettle on the coal stove. A boy, stick in hand, urges a pig onwards; a farmer leads a bullock by its tether. The images are each framed by the doorway for a moment.

Tell the miller, I say, that I'm leaving and I want to thank him for the many hours I've spent here.

Tell the foreigner, the miller replies, that I want him to write a couplet that sums up our many conversations.

I am startled by the miller's request; due to our language differences, barely a word has passed between us.

N would translate the couplet and paint the characters, in black ink on red banners, as I had seen them on the doorways of homes in towns and hamlets throughout the province: the heading, horizontal, above the lintel, and the two lines, vertical on each side of the doorway,

I spend hours trying to compose lines that match the task the miller has set me. The couplet is an exacting art form, an exercise in compressed language. What I hope to say extends far beyond the times I have spent at the watermill.

I want it to capture the passing of the seasons, the people I have met, and my encounters since I first arrived in Huaxi, a hamlet in Guizhou Province, Southwest China, in mid-September

1984, after a two-day journey by train from Beijing.

I awoke on the second morning to farmers working in the rain, thigh-deep in flooded paddies. Solitary figures lumbered up mountain paths, cloaked in rain-capes. Rejuvenated streams burst down steep inclines, and ducks swam in swollen rivers. I was met by officials at Guiyang Station, and driven the final stretch to Guizhou Agricultural College, where I was to teach English to agricultural scientists, and conduct seminars for teachers in the language department. The red identity card the authorities issued had me grandly titled 'foreign expert'.

The college was a world unto itself, the campus located on a rise above the town. Late afternoon, after the day's work was over, I descended a road that ran past workers' cottages, student dormitories and staff apartment blocks into the countryside.

It was autumn when I first set out on the walks. Chilli peppers, corn and grains of rice lay drying on roadsides and in village courtyards in swathes of red, yellow and orange. Terraced paddies rose above fields of yellow rape flowers. Entire fields were given over to plots of vegetables; all was ripe, ready for reaping.

I found alternative routes and became a familiar figure in the hamlets of the Miao and Buyi people, masters in the art of terracing. They invited me into their homes for toasts of *maotai*, a spirit native to Guizhou Province. *Ganbei.* Drink up, they said. I was a novelty, a solitary walker, one of the few foreigners to work in the province in decades.

Whatever route I took, I found my way to a stone bridge straddling the Huaxi River. In the middle of the bridge stood a watermill, and beside it a single willow wreathed by leaf-fall.

The miller invited me in and placed a kettle on the coal stove. He brought the water to the boil, steeped the tea, and when it was done poured it into mugs. He handed one to me, and settled back on a stool with the other.

From time to time a horse-drawn cart clattered past. Women jogged by, balancing tubs on bamboo poles slung across their shoulders. Farmers delivered sacks of grain, which the miller added to those stacked beside the chute leading to the grinding stone. Once done he returned to his stool, rekindled his long-stemmed pipe and continued smoking.

We sat in silence, broken by the laughter of children at play in the river, and the splash of buffalos lazing in the shallows. And all the while, beneath our feet, the steady beat of the waterwheel: *Thoom. Thoom. Thoom.* Round and round, an endless churning.

China was emerging from the Cultural Revolution. As I got to know them, some of my students, aged from eighteen to seventy, would come at night to my apartment and tell me of the trials they had endured during that era.

The country had descended into mass psychosis led by an ageing potentate clinging to power. Chaos engulfed the land, and with it that human capacity for slander and recrimination, bullying and betrayal. Old scores and vendettas were settled many times over, as faction fought faction and the Red Guards roamed the countryside quoting the homilies of their self-appointed Great Helmsman.

The students had been assigned to years of labour in rural areas. Many saw their parents humiliated, imprisoned and exiled to distant farmlands. Loudspeakers resounded with slogans and denunciations. *Bad elements, rich farmers, landlords, counter-revolutionaries and right-wingers* were the five 'black categories'—with *capitalist roaders, traitors* and *foreign agents* the perpetrators of additional felonies. *Intellectuals* completed the roll call as the 'Stinking Ninth'.

The denounced were paraded in the streets and forced to kneel for hours. Placards were hung from their necks. Dunces' hats perched on their heads. Mobs beat them and jeered as they performed the loyalty dance: Chairman Mao is the red sun in our heart, they chanted as they tore apart the lives of former classmates, colleagues and comrades.

The fate of one student embodied the madness. N was a pensive man in his mid-twenties, forever questioning, seeking to fathom life's mysteries. He chose his words carefully, weighing his thoughts before releasing them. We were all caught up in it, he said. Sooner or later we stepped into the quicksand and turned on each other. Once in, there was no way out.

N's father worshipped Mao and was an ardent supporter of revolution. A Red Army soldier in the 1940s, he studied law after liberation and rose to a prominent position in the bureau of public security. He was a decent man, N insists, and he had faith. He followed Mao's injunctions and denounced the cadres he claimed were corrupt. Inevitably, the wheel turned, the accuser became the accused, and the interrogator the victim. N's father was denounced and imprisoned.

A teenage member of the Red Guard, N fell from grace after his father was arrested. He was hounded by classmates, harassed and bullied. Cut off from his father, he was reared by his grandmother. A kindly woman, she was fiercely protective of her grandchild. She was his one constant as the country spiralled into collective madness. Be kind, she told him. But to be kind is not enough, she added. You must be strong if you are to withstand life's fluctuating fortunes.

As a child, N was shy and withdrawn. He dreamt of becoming a soldier in the People's Liberation Army. He was enthralled by films depicting its exploits. He imagined giving up his life on the battlefield and his deeds being known far and wide by the people.

After his father was imprisoned, books became N's solace. He read late into the night, furtively, so as not to arouse suspicion. He developed a passion for ideas, and sought out thinkers and philosophers. He read Rousseau, Voltaire, Goethe and Hegel in Chinese translation, and he came to believe that the writers' craft was forged in hardship. He read Lu Xun, and in his measured prose and subversive stories he found a mentor. He read the Tang and Song dynasty poets and identified with their love of solitude. He read Gorky, Dickens and Hugo and became addicted to novels.

The characters remained in his mind long after he finished reading. They embodied the turmoil he saw about him. Their efforts to make sense of life helped him deal with the imprisonment of his father. His ambitions shifted. He hoped that one day he would become a writer.

Every day, dawn till dusk, the farmers continued to gather the harvest, and in the late afternoons I walked, finding new tracks and retracing familiar ones, making my way to the bridge to sit with the miller; and always the wordless greeting, the kettle on the stove, and the hiss of steam rising, demanding attention like a whining infant. And the two of us, hands warmed by our mugs, seated side by side, in silence.

I would leave the mill in the evening, and make my way beside the river past darkening fields to the town. The streets were crowded. Teams of bullock-drawn carts moved by. Jeeps and trucks wove through the traffic. Weary work-horses hauled carts weighed down with rocks, as the daily roadworks and building construction extended beyond nightfall. Brigades of labourers worked by lamplight in the main street, digging foundations.

Alleys and courtyards lined with cottages gave way to enclaves of apartment blocks, their drabness relieved by pot plants on windowsills and balconies, and the occasional burst of sunflowers. At roadside food stalls and in tea houses, I snacked on slices of fried bean curd filled with hot spices. It was often long dark by the time I arrived back at my campus apartment.

For months on end, seven days a week, bent over in rain, wind and sun, the farmers cleared the fields of rice and corn, sunflowers and rape, draining the fields of their colour. Then it was over, the paddies and fields reduced to dirt and stubble strewn with hayricks. Flocks of geese pecked at leftover grain under the watchful eyes of their keepers. The rice was threshed, husked and bagged. The last stalks of grain lay tied in bundles, and the final yields were ferried from the fields in handcarts and horse-drawn wagons.

It had been a good harvest. The village larders were well

stocked. Red chilli peppers dried in the courtyards. Strings of garlic and corn hung from the roof beams. Pumpkins, spread out on the grey tiled roofs, had turned from green to gold, fully ripened. Bundles of hay were stored in the rafters, in courtyards, and heaped around tree trunks, briquettes stacked in readiness for winter.

A collective sigh settled on the valley. The farmers were still out there, but working at a slower pace: hoeing, digging and ploughing fields for the winter planting. Many fields lay fallow.

N was a frequent guest in my apartment in the cooler nights. He preferred visiting late. His mind was sharpened, he said, by the sense that outside darkness had long fallen. His talk often turned to his early years.

As a child, he was a dreamer. The countryside spoke to him. In his eyes, the stalks of sorghum were nodding their heads and extending their greetings. The rivers, cut deep into the valleys, were pathways to other worlds, sprung from mysterious sources. He roamed the fields, stole into orchards, ate his fill of fruit, and returned home at dusk with his stomach bloated. His grandmother scolded him for overeating.

N's mother was too busy for his persistent questions. But his grandmother listened to him with patience. Her pleasure showed in her eyes, and her concern was reflected in the furrows on her forehead. She called him 'my little treasure' and told him stories of ghosts and ogres, and the rise and fall of dynasties, as they sat by the open doorway on summer nights and by the coal stove in winter. She recalled her tumultuous years as a young revolutionary, but sidestepped the current storms brewing about her.

When a funeral procession passed the doorway, N took fright at the sight of the corpse and the sombre faces of the mourners. Why do we die? he asked. Don't worry, she replied. The wheel of life keeps turning. Life gives way to death, and death paves the way for renewal. You have a long and bright future.

The wheel turned. The Cultural Revolution was over. Mao was dead and the Gang of Four imprisoned. At party gatherings cadres pronounced the new slogans. *Extreme Leftists* were out, and the *Four Modernisations* defined the future. After years of self-imposed isolation, the doors of an empire were opening.

N seized his opportunity. His father remained in prison, and N had assumed the role of family provider. He wanted to be of use to the farmers who worked the terraces above his native village. He studied agriculture, became a research scientist and a teacher of biology and horticulture. He continued his reading and contemplation, and regularly visited his father in prison.

The seasons were turning, the chill intensified, and still I walked to the watermill. I walked as the countryside sank under winter mists and the mountains vanished beneath cloud and drizzle. The willow beside the mill was now bare. Day after day the cloud persisted. I sat beside the miller as the rain beat on the tiled roof, veiling the view from the open doorway. The cold sharpened the senses and the mill interior smelt of damp and hessian.

I headed back to town on muddied pathways. The riverbanks were breaking and the air was thick with the smoke of home fires. Farmers hurried by under plastic sheets. A hunchbacked woman sat between newly ploughed furrows under an umbrella, knitting.

In the town, boys dragged wooden carts heavy with briquettes. Their faces were smeared with coal and their clothes caked with coal dust. Steam rose from woks and stoves. Stallholders in padded jackets remained at work after dark, selling vegetables and herbs, sunflower and pumpkin seeds. I retreated to the tea houses and surveyed the night through the windows and doorways.

And still I walked. Walked until the skies began to crack open. Walked as the rains deluged fields and paddies and turned placid streams into torrents. The hamlets retreated into hibernation, and smoke curled, day and night, from the chimneys. The earth was soaked and the paths dotted with puddles. With each passing day, the hours of darkness lengthened with the approach of the winter solstice.

And through it all, I continued my sojourns at the mill, and through it all the grinding stone continued turning. It could be seen beneath the chute, crushing the harvest into flour, taming my obsessive thoughts into stillness, and the busyness of the day into a quiet punctuated by the beat of the wheel. Round and round, an endless turning.

The first signs of the new season appeared with the preparations for the Spring Festival. People emerged from their rooms and apartments, weaned from the coal stoves they had huddled around on winter evenings. Artisans and tradesmen took their work back into the streets and alleys, and the farmers returned to the fields to harvest the winter crops and prepare the earth for the spring planting.

The smoke of incense rose from family altars and scented the alleys. Lanterns, fashioned as fish and lions, geometric shapes and dragons, trailed from lintels and balconies. Processions of dragons snaked out into the countryside. Exploding crackers marked the beginning of the festive break before a season of back-breaking labour returned in earnest.

Grandmother, why do people fire so many crackers? N asked. My treasure, the sound of crackers can keep ghosts from the door and drive bad luck away, she answered.

The entire country was on the move, returning home for the Spring Festival. I travelled by train with two of my students, N and Q, on the first leg of a three-week journey. We went deep into areas off limits to foreigners. My work card acted as passport.

The carriages were packed with soldiers on leave, farmers smoking hookahs and city workers with their luggage bulging with food and presents. Students in Mao suits sat alongside more daring youths dressed in jeans and leather jackets. Men sat in the aisles, playing cards; children ran wherever they found space, buoyed by a sense of anticipation. At each station, there were joyous reunions and welcomes.

The train disappeared into tunnels blasted through mountainsides, the entries guarded by soldiers. Mountain passes gave way to plains of grazing horses and cattle. Water poured from market-stall awnings and the eaves of thatched homes where children sat in the doorways, crouched over exercise books. Other children propelled tyres through the mud, sending them scuttling down steep pathways.

At each break in the rain, farmers returned to the fields and road workers returned to mixing cement, digging ditches, crushing rock and sifting stone—attacking the mountain with mattocks and mallets, shovels and sledgehammers.

N was more animated than I had ever seen him. He pointed out familiar valleys, and hillsides where stones marked the burial places of ancestors. He told of caves in the earth beneath us, linked by networks of tunnels breaking out into chambers named Cloud Cave, Ballroom, Music Hall. The caves once housed entire families.

We passed hamlets perched on mountain heights and scattered over plateaus and valleys. In one of those hamlets N's grandmother had told her stories. N recounts them now—tales of wise generals and profligate courtiers and of reclusive poets who, millennia ago, retreated to mountain hideaways. Of Tang dynasty poet Han Shan who roamed the peaks alone and carved his poems on bamboo and boulders, temple walls and pavilions.

Some say Han Shan lived in the seventh century. Some say he lived in the eighth, others the ninth. He lived as a recluse in a cliff-side cave with a rock overhang as balcony, a thin layer of grass as his sleeping mat and a stone as pillow. Some say he lived to one hundred and twenty, and others doubt he ever existed.

Han Shan means Cold Mountain, says N. Han Shan lived far from here, but I think of him whenever I travel through mountain country. It is said that he had two sidekicks: Feng-kan, Big Stick; and Shih-te, Pickup.

Feng-kan was over six foot tall. And Shih-te was a ten-year-old boy when Han Shan found him abandoned and took him to a mountain monastery. He was assigned to work in the kitchen, while Feng-kan spent his days in a temple room, hulling rice and chanting scriptures. The three became close friends. They played pranks and made fun of Buddhist and Taoist teachings, even though they practised them.

Some say that Han Shan's poems were written by the three of them. There are three of us, N laughs, but it is not clear who of us is Han Shan, and who are the sidekicks. Maybe we will know by the end of the journey.

Out there, in those lakes, he says, there are salamanders. They are as slippery as eels and as mysterious as your platypus, with the feet of lizards, the heads of turtles and flat toothless mouths that open into pink caverns. They bite and claw farmers who try to catch them to sell as delicacies. They can move fast both on land and in water. Baby fish, the villagers call them, after the cry they make.

There is a story, N says: Not so long ago, many salamanders were lured by villagers from the underground caves they lived in. They scurried from the secure darkness of their hideouts, and scampered up trees in search of a space beyond the reach of their predators. N shakes his head, as if seeing the fugitive salamanders now, chased by their tormentors, somewhere out there beyond the carriage window.

It is twelve kilometres from the station by mountain pass to Q's home town, a world away in another valley. We travelled by jeep up a muddied roadway, our progress hindered by the steep ascent and the approach of darkness. Vehicles returning to the station crawled past. Drivers paused to pass on news of the road conditions. On the sharp descent, the town appeared like a field of lanterns enclosed within the rim of the valley.

We crossed a bridge over a river and were dropped off at Q's home. We deposited our bags and went out immediately. In the streets, we saw posters headed by an image of a skull and crossbones, and bearing the photos of two men who were to be executed the following morning. Their crimes were listed under each photo.

People hurried past, averting their gaze, as if to stop and look for too long would taint them. The condemned men were reminders of the power of the State—and of mortality. We must purge crime from all corners of this country, proclaimed banners stretched across the streets. Let it serve as a warning. Stray from the path and this is the fate that awaits you.

We slept that night in Q's home. I woke in the early hours to howling dogs and crowing roosters. The rain resumed. It drummed on the roof and against the shutters. Somewhere nearby, two men were spending their last night among the living. As the first light seeped in, there arose the sound of a pig being slaughtered. Its screams were human, rising in intensity.

I looked out of the window at the courtyard. Tied down by ropes, the pig fought with ferocity. The shouting of the men holding it down grew louder. A fierce battle was taking place, with an inevitable outcome. Finally, the animal fell silent. Its suffering was at an end. For the doomed prisoners, however, the journey to the execution grounds had not yet started.

~

Six years ago, Q's father lay dying. In his final days, party officials and farmers filed by his bed to farewell him. They sat by his side, drank tea and recalled times past like ageing veterans at a reunion. In what would be his last night, Q's father roused himself from his bed and made his way on unsteady feet to the table. He asked his wife and children to sit beside him as he wrote his last will and testament.

His life had spanned the final years of the Long March, the Japanese occupation, civil war and the triumph of revolution. He had wept at Mao's proclamation of the People's Republic and had lived through Mao's death and with it the death throes of the Cultural Revolution. He had been in his prime in the 1950s, the springtime of revolution, when comrades danced waltzes and tangos and when true believers devoted their lives to the collective. He had endured the Great Leap Forward, the dark years of famine, and the descent into chaos and recrimination, denunciation and rehabilitation. And he had survived it all, each swing of the pendulum, each dictum. He was a foot soldier, a party functionary, self-effacing.

Q was, like his father, a loyalist and a battler. Unlike his father, he had the pallor of a man who spent his days in study. His face was smooth, and his hair neatly cut. He was invariably dressed in a regulation blue Mao suit, spotless and pressed, and he began each day with his shoes polished. Despite all that had transpired, he too remained a true believer. His goal as an agricultural scientist was to serve the people, he said, as his father had before him; and, as had generations before them, shaped by a far older convention of subservience to dynastic powers and emperors.

The framed testament hung on the wall beneath a photo of Q's father, taken in his final months. His face is gaunt and his gaze direct, touched by an air of sadness and forbearance. Q helped his father dissolve the inkstick in a bowl of water. He placed the brush in his hand and steadied the parchment as he wrote the sentiments he was so anxious to bequeath him.

Q watched the ink flowing from his brush, and the characters taking shape as the ink dried, assuming permanence. He was taken by his father's unhurried composition of the words that would outlive him. The characters formed vertical columns. Despite Q's assistance, the hand that painted them remained unsteady, as was to be expected of a man who had risen from his deathbed. This had given the characters a unique quality prized in the art of calligraphy.

A person's character, said N, as he stood beside us in front of the testament, is indicated in the manner of their calligraphy. It reveals whether they are open or secretive, outgoing or withdrawn, weak or decisive. You can tell whether the strokes were applied in a state of confusion or harmony, whether in haste or calm deliberation, in stiff control or wild abandon. The characters applied by Q's father, N said, indicated his steadfastness in the face of adversity.

Q translated the document for me and wrote the English words in fountain pen. He sat at the table at which his father had written his testament, bent over an exercise book, intensely focused. He applied pressure on the down strokes and paused after each sentence. The letters leaned to the right in perfect unison. The ink could be seen drying as each letter was written.

Q had refined his English script through many hours of practice, copying the letters over and again from templates of perfection. He saw writing as an art form regardless of which script he was using. The neat strokes reflected the character of a man who took pride in following correct procedure.

Yet, there were hints of something else—modest flourishes in some of the letters, and in the tails of the g's and j's, the y's and p's. Perhaps one day he would abandon his adherence to routine, and embark on journeys to unknown destinations.

The document is headed *Testament.* The first people Q's father addresses are his comrades, followed by family, conforming to a prescribed order of priorities:

> *Respected, loyal revolutionaries, family, friends, Comrade T, my dear Q, X, H, J and P—my children. There is no living without death, but no death without living. Everyone dies. Death is also one of the joys of life.*
>
> *During the period of my illness, I have often reflected on my forty years of revolutionary work, my political thoughts, and my way of life. I feel that my actions have always been guided by the wishes of the party, the people and my conscience. I welcome peacefully the coming of my last day: I have no tears or sorrow, or any pain or terror before death.*
>
> *The leaders of the government, good friends, general comrades, residents of the town and peasants have come to see*

me in my final weeks, and extended their regards to me. The Party, people and comrades have offered their respect, so I feel that I will die happily.

In response to the Party's great and correct call that our work must be guided by the Four Modernisations of socialism, I shall take the method of cremation. My bone ash will be put in a plastic bag, and hence save a little money for the Party, and a little material wealth for society. I consider this as my last contribution to the Four Modernisations.

My simple coffin will be an old cotton uniform, a pair of old socks, a pair of old shoes and an old straw hat. I hope that Comrade T will faithfully do this in accordance with my wishes. If any changes are made because of affection for the old ideas, it will be false to our love and a shame for me. I ask the leaders of the government, and my affectionate friends, to carry this out.

After my cremation, half of my bone ash will be carried back to my home town and will be cast over the place where I last worked for the Party, to encourage the farmers to continue the experiment of no-ploughing rice method.

Signed: Y's last words for his family.

Q's father saw himself as a humble comrade. He would not allow himself any self-indulgence. He was much like my own imprisoned father, observed N, but with less guile, and on a lower rung in the party hierarchy. Unlike N's father, Q's father would never have risen to high office. He had remained a party functionary. My father, said N, was far more ambitious, and there came a time when his ambition got the better of him. In retrospect, from his prison cell, he would have envied Q's father.

In the evening, we sat with Q's mother, his siblings and their spouses, nieces and nephews around a knee-high circular table, constructed around a charcoal burner. Embedded in the earth floor, and enclosed in guard rails, it heated the room and warmed the food that simmered in a hotpot that sat on a grate above the glowing embers. The rice wine flowed and the family was at ease, engaged in idle chatter. There was no mention of the pending executions.

The following evening, there appeared a sequence of photos on display boards depicting the execution, along with a skull and crossbones and the words: 'This is the fate that awaits criminals.' The condemned men are pictured standing in the courtroom docks as the judge passes the verdict. Then they appear at a town meeting, where they are denounced and their crimes are recounted. They are paraded on the back of a truck en route to the place of execution. Bystanders look on passively. They are participants in a set piece. The prisoners' fate was as certain as that of the pig on the previous evening, trussed up for slaughter.

They are on their knees, heads bowed, with the firing squad lined up, guns aimed at their hearts, the order to shoot imminent. Then slumped on the ground, their hands tied, knees drawn to their chests. Their bodies are curled in on themselves, as if seeking a return to the womb, maternal affection. A red cross blots out the name of each executed man, accompanied by the inscription: 'The criminal has been wiped out.'

Posted just hours after the men's death, the black and white images seemed to already belong to a distant past. The men's faces haunted me: fear and humiliation tempered by resignation. Expressions as fixed as the sentiments in Q's father's final testament.

We continued our journey by jeep. High above the town we stopped, stepped out and looked down on the valley. The town was situated between the two branches of a river. On the upper slopes stood a cluster of Buddhist temples and pavilions, interspersed by stone steps carved into the mountain. And, higher up, a spread of tombstones and a recent burial site, marked by a wreath of flowers and white cloths, frayed after days of exposure.

From our viewpoint, the dwellings were a congregation of tiled roofs flanked by pebbled riverbanks spread with sheets and clothing. The slap of women beating clothes could be faintly heard about us. Multi-storeyed wooden houses looked down on the river from stone ramparts, well clear of the flood line. Boatmen poled barges laden with barrels of fuel, fruit and vegetables.

I was overtaken by a vague sadness; and an impulse to remain here, a foreigner who had strayed off the path, lured by the stillness. A convoy of army vehicles eased their way over a bridge. People moved unhurriedly about their business. Below us, an enclosed world and a sense of time slowing, and above us, a vista of wind-driven clouds and snow-capped pinnacles.

And beyond, intimations of valley after concealed valley in a province where, for millennia, those who had fallen out of favour were banished from Imperial courts and the centres of power. Until this day, Guizhou Province had served as a place of exile for outcasts and renegades, the falsely accused, and the outspoken, 'dangerous elements'. Beyond sight and marooned in the outposts of empire.

We were dwarfed by a dramatic landscape, as insignificant as figures in a Chinese painting. Everything seemed poised, at a standstill. We did not want to move. Gusts of cold wind reared up from the valley and, reaching above the sound of the wind, N's voice, reciting Han Shan:

I climb the road to Cold Mountain.
The road to Cold Mountain that never ends.
The valleys are long and strewn with stones,
The stream broad and banked with grass.
Moss is slippery, though no rain has fallen,
Pines sigh, but it isn't the wind.
Who can break from the snares of the world
And sit with me among the white clouds?

We continued our journey by bus, passing hamlets of clay houses and thatched cellars storing grain and sweet potato. We spent nights in village inns or with the families of students returned home for the festival. The bus laboured on the heights past farmers climbing the steep slopes between the terraced paddies.

The passengers were lulled into slumber by the drone of the engine and the faint sound of an infant singing. The reverie was jolted by a baby screaming, as if she had suddenly woken and sensed the immensity of the world about her: precipices at the edge of the earth plummeting into a frightening infinity. Even those who had lived here their entire lives now seemed in awe of the scale of the landscape.

They had left the comfort and commerce of the valley and were in thrall to places that could not be tamed, despite their efforts to domesticate them. Again, I was overcome by a sense of time slowing and the temptation to vanish. *Who can break from the snares of the world/ And sit with me among the white clouds?*

In the depths of a valley, on the banks of a river, in a two-storey wooden house, lived a stone carver. He worked at a bench strewn with files, chisels, knives and gouges, mallets and hammers. As he worked he told us his story.

There were three families who practised the craft of inkstand carving in the valley. Each possessed its unique style dating back centuries. He practised a style known as *Dragons Playing for Treasure*. He had displayed an aptitude for carving as a young boy, and was apprenticed to his uncle at nineteen.

For the first three years, he cleaned his uncle's rooms, washed and cooked and ran errands. He was not allowed to handle the tools. He would hide and watch his uncle at work, in secret. He set himself a rigorous program of exercise to build up strength in his hands, shoulders and forearms. When he was finally allowed to practise, he worked many hours perfecting his craft, emulating his uncle's movements. He picked up the skills quickly.

In time, he was judged to have attained enough mastery to practise alone. From his hands, there flowed figures of dragons and tigers doing battle, phoenixes rearing towards the sun, serpents swimming, turtles paddling, birds perched on plum blossoms and goldfish at play in turbulent waters.

When he worked, the carver inhabited the worlds of his creations. Each line incised in the stone followed its prescribed path, sculpting forms handed down through generations. Yet there was also something of the carver's own, individual lines shaped by the living hand while in harness to something greater.

When he raised his head, he was greeted by the sight of paddies alternating with forested mountainside. The world about him and the world of his creations were one. Each was of earth and stone, changing over the years, taking shape, and evolving, albeit at a different pace, one measured in hours, the other in millennia. The seasons turned and returned but the craft, and the tradition that upheld it, remained constant.

The stone carver paused, looked up, and cast his eyes over the mountain. It is simple, he said. The work speaks for itself. Then he fell silent and returned to the carving.

When the Cultural Revolution engulfed the country, the stone carver's work was forced underground. It was condemned as an indulgence. He no longer warranted the stipend he received from the Ministry of Culture. He was directed to teach primary-school children and to work in the farmlands.

As he worked he flexed his fingers and imagined himself back at his table. He saw the hoe as a carving instrument and the field's boulders as material. He saw the muddied farmlands as ink, variable in consistency and texture, ranging from damp earth to liquid. In the ploughed fields, he made out the calligrapher's brushstrokes, the artistry.

He does not wish to dwell on those times. They have passed, he says. They will return, and they will pass again. Humans will always lose their way, come to their senses, and lose their way again. There will always be tyrants to be overthrown and tyrants plotting to replace them.

As he works, he rarely misses a beat, even as he changes implements, picking them out from the arsenal lined up on the table. Each new line carved, each serpent's scale chipped, each groove is fine and intricate. He dismisses recent history with a wave of his hands. He dwells in a more distant past, shaped by the conventions of his craft and a lineage of antecedents.

This is what he loves speaking of most, the craft. His eyes light up. He pauses to talk of the finer points. The ink stone he is carving, he says, is one of the Four Treasures of the Study. It ranks alongside the writing brush, the inkstick and the parchment. While labouring in the fields, he had imagined the earth as a parchment, and in the summer months, the hardened dirt and rock as the base of an ink stone. The summer showers were flows of ink, filling the furrows.

Each of the Four Treasures is a separate craft, he tells us. The rate of absorption and quality of the paper evolved through experimentation. The inkstick and brush handles were carved in the shapes of lotus leaves, fruit and flowers, fish and animals. The designs were symbolic and an end in themselves, adding to the pleasure of the calligrapher.

To be dedicated to the craft was a form of madness and a retreat from the world. The Tang and Song dynasty poets understood it, he says, and they concluded that there are things that can only be known in silence. Han Shan knew it, as one who had withdrawn from the world. He carved his poems into rock faces.

When people meet Han Shan,
They all say he's crazy.
His look doesn't attract the gaze
And he is wrapped up in a cloth gown.
I speak and they don't understand.
When they speak, I keep silent,
So I tell people,
Come and visit me on Cold Mountain.

We journeyed on, the three of us, Han Shan and his sidekicks, Feng-kan and Shih-te. One night, in a mountain inn, we were joined at dinner by a teacher, a middle-aged man of the Dong people. He listened intently to our tales of travel, and the following morning he joined us. He left home with little money and without informing his family, and for six days he attached himself to us. He was dressed in a shabby suit, and as thin as a beanpole. We dubbed him the 'Wine Monster' since he was given to drinking binges.

We stayed overnight in a mountain town and after the evening meal, made our way to the workers' club. Long-haired youths in tight jeans, cowboy hats, leather boots and Hawaiian shirts danced disco. Their attire and dancing were modest acts of rebellion. The tables stood by the walls, forming a circle around the dance floor. The Wine Monster sat with us, draining glass after glass of wine in a frenzy.

You are lucky, he slurred. You are passing through, but I must stay and return to my teaching. Year after year, my students graduate and leave for distant places and higher studies, while I stay back here. Curse my luck. Curse my fate. Curse the mountains. They are strangling me. He runs a finger across his neck in a cutting gesture.

The Wine Monster stumbles from the table to the dance floor, hips jiggling, spindly legs prancing in jerky movements. He lowers his arms towards his feet, then stretches them above his head and leaps up, arms fully extended. His steps lengthen, his movements become more expansive. The young men back away and the circle of onlookers widens.

His hand moves from his heart to the air in a gesture of adoration for Chairman Mao, in a mock version of the loyalty dance, which he had performed during the Cultural Revolution as a member of a propaganda team travelling from village to village. He weaves his way back to the table, resumes his drinking and breaks out in a drunken rendition of 'Chairman Mao Is the Red Sun in Our Hearts'.

We leave the hall and make our way back to the hotel. The Wine Monster is unmindful of the chill; his down coat is unzipped. He strides ahead and comes to a stop halfway across a bridge. He places his hands on the rails, leans over and yells at the water. He lifts his head and screams at the skies and the upper slopes of the mountain. His voice echoes and his slim shadow darts over the roadway.

He turns to us as we approach and sings: 'Chairman Mao is the red sun in our hearts', the same line, over and again, in the same unhinged melody. People pass by. No one takes any notice.

The following day he is contrite and melancholic. He directs us in a succession of busses deep into Dong country, to the towns and hamlets of his people. Clusters of tiled roofs rise above riverbanks in isolated valleys, creeping up the lower slopes, beneath a succession of fields and terraces. In the centre of each settlement stands a drum tower. It rises above the double-storey wooden houses and is topped by a roof structure with multiple eaves curving upwards.

The towers are inspired by the shape of giant cedars, says the Wine Monster. He has assumed the role of guide. He is alert and inflated with a sense of purpose. They were built without nails or rivets, he says. My people are master architects and builders. We know how to transform our beloved trees into meeting places.

He is warming to his task. His reticence is gone. His eyes are alight and his face has softened. He is at ease in his surroundings; his burden has momentarily lifted. He speaks a rapid-fire English, and is surprisingly eloquent for one who acquired the language by rote learning and listening to BBC broadcasts on shortwave radio.

The towers are supported by sixteen wooden pillars, he says. The village elders summon the residents by drum to meetings. The four central pillars represent the four seasons. The other twelve represent the months of the year. We worship big trees and I worship wine, he laughs. And in Dong villages wine flows like water.

We approach the Wine Monster's home village late in the afternoon. We step from the bus and are drawn through the streets by the refrains of a Dong opera. The musicians perform on a podium in the central square in front of the drum tower. The villagers sit on benches, their eyes riveted on the performers.

Children run about. Pigs and geese wander in the mud, and babies nestle on their mothers' backs in cloth papooses.

Mid-opera, the skies open. The rain pours, and the water rises, gushing through the alleys, carving rivulets. The villagers run to the drum tower, seeking the warmth of the log fire that burns permanently in a pit within the four central pillars. The touring opera company continues its performance. The voices are muffled by the downpour. The Wine Monster is tranquil. Drink quietly, he says. This is the way of my people.

It was dark by the time the opera ended. We hurried on slippery paths to the rooms assigned to us, and slept the sound sleep of the weary traveller to the drumming of rain on the roofs of the village; and woke to the sounds of the mountain shedding water. The roads were closed. Frost glazed the fallow earth and rooftops.

This is how it was for several days, leaving us stranded. There was no sky to be seen. Cloud descended on the lower slopes and hung in the valley. Our gloom was dispelled by hours of feasting hosted by the village headmen and a foray, under the guidance of the Wine Monster, to a Flower Bridge.

A masterpiece, he enthused. The bridge columns and planks were interlocked tightly, and the bridge was covered with roof tiles engraved with flowers. Dragons, phoenixes, snakes and tigers curled around the wooden pillars. The ceiling was adorned with peacocks, and the walls with paintings of ox fights, scenes of battle and of daily life: villagers hunting, weaving and playing musical instruments.

A masterpiece, the Wine Monster repeated. Hours later, back in the village, on the earth floor beneath the tower, he was dancing: the swaying of his hips and the flow of his arms learned in childhood and refined by tradition, a sharp contrast to the mock loyalty dance he had performed at the workers' club days earlier.

His mood had shifted in the past two days from despair to elation. The nights flowed with the dialect of the Dong, and with young men and women passing by in the darkness, their laughter approaching and fading. And the four of us, seated by the fire in the Drum Tower with the men and women of the village. Drinking quietly.

We left by bus, a band of four. The slopes were clothed in damp green forest. Ice clung to shrubs and pylons; snow slid from the branches and dropped silently beneath them. Wood burners lit up the windows of roadside houses. Giant waterwheels churned in mountain streams, while fishermen spread their nets in shallow waters. A funeral procession moved by, mourners dressed in white, carrying bouquets of paper flowers.

The spell of our stay with the Dong was broken. The Wine Monster sat alone, flagon in hand, refusing company. Brooding. His mood was as dark as the soaked landscape. The mountains are strangling me, he slurred. You are the red sun that shines in our heart, he sang, then lapsed back into a sullen silence. And in the evening, after we had stopped for the night, he vanished, leaving us as he had joined us, without reason or forewarning.

That night, I dreamt: Two men on motorcycles are riding up a mountain trail. The road is covered in ice and hoarfrost. It runs alongside a sheer drop, disappearing far below into the depths of a valley. The men are confident in their movements. They turn onto a rock ledge and accelerate in circles, carving ruts into the ice surface; then hurtle towards the edge of the cliff and over it.

They look up as they fall, detached from their motorcycles. I stand above the chasm and watch them. On their faces, expressions of fear and wonder. One lands feet-first in a muddy bog, the other lands on his back beside him. For a moment, the men are inert. Then they begin to move. They struggle to their feet, look up at the cliff and shake their heads in disbelief. They are elated, and I am tempted. Perhaps I can do this. Dare. Leap. Surrender to the mountain.

We travelled on. One morning we came across a wedding party led by a band of musicians. Relatives carried furniture and bedding. A truck, loaded with guests, inched through the narrow streets. We followed the parade to the upper slopes. The women were gathered in one house, the men in another. The bride's home was decorated with yellow banners painted with the double happiness symbol. A couplet on red paper framed the doorway.

N translated: Above the lintel: 'A long prosperous marriage'. On the left-hand side: 'Work together with skilful hands to make the rivers and mountains beautiful'. And on the right: 'People in love with each other carry the world on their iron shoulders'. And if the marriage fails, laughs N, there is always the way of Han Shan and the retreat to Cold Mountain.

For Weipo there is no retreat to the mountain. Her grandson

meets us mid-afternoon at the bus station. B is another student of mine home for the Spring Festival. He guides the three of us through the town centre. The main street is lined with government buildings giving way to streets that narrow into muddy alleys.

B points out the homes of relatives and former school friends. A group of teenage boys play pool at an outdoor table. Flocks of geese forage on clay paths. Piglets cling to the teats of a sow stretched out in the mud on a vacant allotment, and dogs lie in the dirt eyeing us lazily. And, at the door of his house, Weipo, B's maternal grandmother, is waiting.

She stands in front of her clan like the leader of a delegation, wearing a black headscarf, a navy-blue Mao suit and slippers. Children peak out from behind her, shy and excited by the arrival of the foreigner. She embraces me. I am a teacher of her grandson, and that is all she need know. I am welcome.

Weipo leads me into the house, and her children and grandchildren trail behind her. She walks with a stoop, but there is strength in her gaze and pride in her bearing. She ushers us into the room she has set aside for the three guests. Members of the clan spill through the doorway. They laugh and comment. This is a spectacle, and I am the object.

This is where we will stay for the remaining days of the journey, content to be down from the mountain: going out daily to the valley, and feasting each night on glutinous rice, boiled chicken, pork in sweet sauce, mushroom stuffed with beef, and pickled cabbage. Fired up by toasts of white wine and the nightly ritual, as Weipo's newborn great-grandchild, *Xiao Taiyang,* Little

Sun, is swaddled in woollens of red, white and yellow and passed around the room from person to person like a bobbing balloon to her destination, the arms of Weipo.

Weipo is the matriarch. She is continually on the move, releasing hens from their coops, gathering eggs from wood-baskets, planting and tending, feeding wood into the stove and hanging stringed sausages alongside strips of pork from the beams of the kitchen. Her life is centred on her brood of descendants.

Her territory embraces the homes of her neighbours. They come to her for advice. She is expert in home remedies, the nursing of animals and the rearing of children. She is the arbiter of domestic disputes and petty squabbles. She presides over a maze of alleys and wooden cottages, and navigates her confined kingdom, step by step, breath by breath, from the kitchen to the room where the family gathers, and out to the garden, eyes cast downwards, ensuring the safety of her footing. From time to time she lifts her head and looks up at the ranges that encircle the valley. She knows what lies beyond. She has no need to venture further.

She had come through the mountains as a child, with her family, seventy years ago, in search of a life beyond the impoverishment of their home village. When they laid their eyes on the valley, its fertile soils and the protection the mountains afforded, they knew they had found what they were looking for. Weipo has lived in this house ever since.

Over the years she has seen the hamlet expand into a town. She does not wish to dwell on the past. There have been dark times and good times, is all she will say. Despite it all, she views her life as a steady ascent out of poverty. And now this unexpected late-life gift: with festival days restored and, with them, the return of family members from all corners of the province. She knows they will journey back each year, by bus and train, in trucks and four-wheel drives, making their way through the mountains, as she did, seven decades earlier.

On festival nights, we cross the river on a passenger canoe and walk past fishing boats lying on the banks beneath banyan trees. We climb the lower reaches of the foothills above the town. The government buildings in the centre of town are ablaze with new year decorations. On either side of the river, wooden houses give way to farmlands in the expansive valley. From this distance, the town appears to huddle at the base of the towering mountain.

It is the Year of the Ox, and Weipo lights the candles and incense in front of the altar that sits on a dressing table. The centrepiece is a statuette of Guanyin, the goddess of compassion. She is flanked by Lao Tse and a fat laughing Buddha. Chubby infants crawl over his shoulders and pot belly. On the wall above the altar, a poster of a tiger, edged by the lines of a couplet: *The Tiger runs like lightning. And this lightning is more beautiful than the colours of the rainbow.*

Against the opposite wall of the room stands a television on which there sits a bowl of plastic chrysanthemums. Above it there are posters of the Monkey King and Premier Chou En Lai presenting a bouquet of flowers to Chairman Mao. Their complexions are airbrushed smooth and their heads encircled by halos. Weipo makes her way outside as the evening fireworks erupt.

Her day of work is done. She sits on a stool in the clay street in front of the house. She lifts her head. Her gaze extends beyond the streets, beyond the festivities, to the mountain. She closes her eyes and listens to the murmur of conversation, the slap of cards at outdoor tables, the explosions of crackers, and the weary cries of peddlers selling their dwindling supplies of snacks and fireworks. She dozes off and awakes to the crowing of roosters disoriented by the lights blazing post-midnight.

Tomorrow the farewells will begin, family gatherings at the bus station, with stoic embraces before the return journeys to colleges and workplaces. But at this moment, winter and spring are finely balanced, and the mountains a circle of guardians shielding the valley from outside intrusions.

Weipo opens her eyes and turns to me. Her habitual sternness is gone, and I glimpse a radiance I have seldom encountered. Her eyes are alight with wonder, and her gaze casts warmth on all it touches. She is both childlike and ageless; she has vanquished the boundaries between dream and reality. She lifts her hands to receive Little Sun, wraps her in her arms and rocks her to sleep. She has no need to leave the valley. No desire to be elsewhere.

On our return to Huaxi I resume my walks into the countryside. Families are back at work in the fields. The ranges have regained their coating of green, and the parklands their canopies of plum and peach blossoms. Chill winds give way to intimate breezes and violent rainstorms. The Huaxi River overflows its banks and floods the rice paddies. On the willow beside the watermill, buds are appearing.

From a distance, all is serene and interdependent, symmetry and movement, the landscape a tableau of farmer and plough, paddies and fields of rape flower. But close-up all is brute force and labour, mud and shit, muscle and tendon strained to the limit. The beasts can be heard snorting and rasping. Farmers, stripped to the waist, thigh-deep in mud, exhort their yoked horses to keep moving. Pleading, cajoling, they will them on, at times lovingly, at others beating them and shouting. An ageing farmer bent under a heavy load of grain struggles up a steep path. A young child pushes a cart piled high with the last of the winter harvest. A bullock gasps for breath as its owner whips it in a frenzy.

This is how it is, N says, when he accompanies me on one of my walks. And why we study, bend our backs to our books, in search of ways to ease the burden. N's language, and his formal expression are of another era, partly acquired from textbooks. By now, I am accustomed to his way of speaking. I have met many others like him. His sentiments reflect the aspirations of a man raised by an ethos of sacrifice and service. Despite it all—his father's imprisonment, the cruelty and chaos he had witnessed, and his years of ostracism—N remains a true believer.

As with the countryside, so it was with the entire country, but in reverse. Viewed from afar, the revolution had been betrayed and reduced to accusation, rampage and murder. Yet after months of living here, I begin to see the nuances and the humanity of those who had endured it, reflected in tales of exile and struggle and embodied in N's childhood dream:

I saw a big bird flying. My arms turned into wings. I flew towards a tree and perched there. I saw several boys playing on the grasslands. I shouted to them. They heard my voice and told me to fly down and play with them. I did not want to do this. The boys were upset. They picked up stones and threw them at me. To avoid them, I flew back into the skies. I flew for a long time and grew anxious. I wanted to fly back home but I was too tired. I fell back to earth. My back hurt. I woke up and found myself lying on the floor beside my bed. I stood up, felt the ground beneath me, and kept moving.

It is twenty minutes by bus to Guiyang, the province capital. Gangs of labourers are at work on building sites on a Sunday morning. The streets are dense with factories and high-rise apartments. A pall of black smoke drifts above the city. The pavements throng with shoppers. Iron railings prevent the crowds from spilling onto the roadway.

Through open doorways, women and children can be seen shaping sheets of metal into woks and watering cans. Carpenters work in dimly lit garages. Barbers stand on the pavement, clipping the hair of customers seated on footstools, alongside tailors plying their trade on sewing machines. Booksellers stand behind stacks of paperbacks.

Amid this tumult, I come upon the Little Gentleman. We collide as he steps onto the pavement from the Children's Palace: a funfair of carousels, slides and monkey bars. He wears a weathered grey suit and a white shirt neatly tucked into his trousers. Cloth patches reinforce the jacket elbows. His shoes are worn but well-polished. He is chubby, his weight offset by his alert eyes and brisk movement. His hair is a crewcut black and he walks with short rapid steps, back straight, shoulders open. He is ten-years-old, but carries himself like an adult.

He is by my side as we board a bus. He speaks fluent English and has assumed the role of interpreter. Inside the bus he seems smaller, in contrast to the adults leaning over him. The seats are taken, and passengers crowd the aisles and entrances. Bodies register each movement. We are like matches in a box, says one passenger. I think we should envy the matches for the breathing space they have, says another.

The Little Gentleman and I step off the bus together. He guides me through narrow streets, past cottages with grey slate roofs and wooden houses hard up against the concrete walls of three-storey apartment blocks. A man's face, ghostly white, appears at a window; a parrot shrieks in a cage suspended over a doorway. Chickens cackle in coops clustered on several balconies. Between blocks we glimpse mountain peaks towering on the city's outskirts. The air is acrid with smoke; Guiyang is a city that struggles to withstand the daily onslaught of industrial waste and congested living.

We come to a halt at a housing block with the drab appearance common to Mao-era dwellings. The Little Gentleman leads me to a second-floor apartment. He lives with his grandparents. His parents, high-school teachers, live and work in a distant town.

The living room is furnished with armchairs, stools and cushions. A small bookshelf displays a four-volume digest of world literature. On one wall hangs a framed ivory carving of a flock of cranes in flight, their necks extended. On the wall opposite is a poster of Renoir's veiled woman. The room speaks of poverty, but also homeliness.

In the centre of the room there sits a coal stove, with pots of salted beef, rice noodles, steamed vegetables and chilli. The Little Gentleman joins his grandparents in ferrying dishes to and from the stove. He places a bowl of sweets, plates and cups on a low table beside a vase of chrysanthemums.

When we are settled, Grandmother does the talking, while Grandfather sits back in his armchair with his arms folded. She is fluent in English, with barely a hint of the Chinese syntax of most local speakers. As she talks she gazes at the coal stove. From time to time her gaze shifts to the poster of the veiled woman, as if drawing on it as a reference point. Fragments of story appear between lapses into silence, backed by the murmur of chatter in neighbouring apartments.

It was in 1945 that Grandmother met the English woman. Mrs F had lost her husband to war and had come to Guizhou Province to teach English. She made her way to this little-known city in search of anonymity. She talked little of the past, save to say that she wanted to do something of worth far from the battlefields that had left her a widow.

History, Mrs F was soon to learn, is ridden with ironies. The war was, it seemed, over in Europe, but in China it had not ended. The Japanese had been driven out, but the country resumed the bloody civil conflict that had been, in part, suspended in the face of a common enemy.

Grandmother pauses. The clouds have parted. A band of sun slips in through the window and lights up her face and the Renoir poster. She closes her eyes and takes in the warmth. In contrast to the tumultuous events she is recounting, she is calm and tranquil. Her husband appears older, and his laughter, when it breaks out, is deeper.

The couple has weathered many crises, and the years have taught them the art of acceptance. It is there, in Grandfather's easy silences, and in the quiet cadences of Grandmother's speech. The weight of history, and the suffering it had wrought, had honed their patience; they had adapted to their fate and learnt to live with the twists of fortune.

These qualities have been instilled in the Little Gentleman. He is precocious in his patience and his air of cheerful obedience. He pours the tea into porcelain cups, content to do his grandparents' bidding. His movements are confident and compact; he is well practised in the art of hospitality.

Mrs F lived in Guiyang for three years. She stayed on when Mao made his triumphant entry into Beijing and proclaimed the birth of the Peoples Republic of China. The country was swept up in euphoria. The fighting was finally over and the nation united. This is how it had been in the Middle Kingdom for millennia: periods of fighting and disintegration, followed by the consolidation of a new dynasty. The revolution would surely deliver them.

Mrs F worked as a volunteer teacher at a primary school. She said little about her past, and much of what she did say Grandmother has long forgotten. Within months of the proclamation of the Republic, Mrs F announced her time in Guiyang was over. The country had regained its independence and was forging a new identity. It was time to return to England.

This, at least, is how Grandmother remembers it, along with the sense of loss she felt on the afternoon her friend left. She recalls it with clarity: the bus ride to Guiyang Station, the silent walk to the platform, and the clamour of the crowds as she helped her friend lift her suitcases into the carriage.

Mrs F settled in her window seat and waved as the train drew away from the platform. Grandmother remained, her eyes focused on the rails, as if trying to fix that point where the train vanished. She was overcome by a wave of envy. Mrs F was disappearing into a wide world, while she remained enclosed in a landlocked city. She felt the weight of it as she made her way through the shabby streets of Guiyang to a flat made somehow smaller by her friend's absence.

Grandmother was now competent in English, her fluency born out of conversation. She taught English for twenty years in a Guiyang middle school and enjoyed the process of refining her students' phrasing and diction.

It was, she says, like watching ink dry on parchment, the words in her students' speech assuming greater clarity. Learning a new language was an act of persistence and the rewards, though slow in coming, were enduring. She loved teaching, but her career was cut short by the Cultural Revolution.

Grandmother speaks of the events matter of factly. She was beaten by her students, paraded through the school and forced to crawl like a dog as they berated her. The placard dangling from her neck branded her a counter-revolutionary, a spy and a decadent.

Her former friendship with a foreigner, and her fluency in English, had made her suspect. She hid her language books for fear her students would burn them. She got rid of the correspondence and documents that would have associated her with the English woman. As anticipated, her students ransacked her flat in search of incriminating evidence.

Grandmother pauses and returns her gaze to the framed poster. I wish to travel, she says, changing the subject. I wish to go to England and see Mrs F. She had long lost touch with her foreign friend, but hoped she was still living. She had two former classmates who had left Guiyang years ago and were living in London.

They will be my starting point, she says, and from there I can begin my search. She is saving money for the journey. Once a month she visits a sister in a provincial town where she buys fresh beef. She dries and salts the meat, and returns to Guiyang where she sells it to local businesses.

The English woman loved Guiyang, she says. She would say: Guiyang is a well-kept secret, a city concealed in a forgotten valley. I am so far from everywhere, no one need know I exist. She was a good woman, says Grandmother. She asked for little, worked diligently, and did not judge others.

Grandmother has no photos of her. Not one. Her face had disappeared when the train pulled out of view from the Guiyang Station, and the few photos she did have were destroyed by her rampaging students. No matter how hard she tried to retain the image, as the years went by she lost her picture of her.

A year ago, Grandmother was out walking when she passed a stall selling posters of paintings: Chinese landscapes and works of the Western canon. She was arrested by the poster of the veiled woman. There was something familiar about her. She was drawn to its sombre beauty, the muted colours, and something else: the woman and her stance evoked a lost memory, more precisely, the impression of a memory. She could not quite place it.

When she arrived home she leaned the framed print against the wall, stepped back and contemplated it. It was not so much a physical resemblance, but the woman's elusiveness. The portrait was a study of transience. It evoked the fading dream that Mrs F's three-year stay had come to be.

The veiled woman has become the dominant presence; she commands our attention. Her face is turned away. She is on a threshold, about to step into the cold, perhaps at nightfall. She is slightly huddled as if uncertain of what awaits her. Behind the veil can be seen an earring, shaped as a flower with black petals. A bow of blue, white and pink below her chin adds a touch of colour, as too the right-hand cuff, and her hat with its brown and white feather.

The thumb and forefinger of the right hand appear to be holding a small object, perhaps a purse. All that can be seen of the left hand is the thumb, and that too is barely visible. Her thick shawl suggests winter. The entire painting is veiled in a green darkness, tempered by the light streaming through the windows.

One day, says Grandmother, addressing me directly, you

will remember Guizhou as my friend did, as a place where you spent time and then left to get on with your life elsewhere. Your friends will accompany you to the station and help you with your luggage. Until the last moment you will be a living presence, as they will be to you, standing face to face, making promises.

Then you will step aboard and settle into your seat. Already you will be elsewhere. You will continue to wave, and you will be sad at your parting, but that will be outweighed by your anticipation of the journey ahead of you. You will see your friends' faces fade from view and see the mountains close ranks behind you. And they will remain on the platform long after the final wave, staring at the empty tracks, transfixed by that moment when a living presence begins to give way to memory.

The clear image of those you have known here will wane, but from time to time, unexpectedly, you will dream of them. Scenes will form before you, perhaps of the countryside, and the way the mountains press in on this city, perhaps of your brief time in this room, and the afternoon light settling on the veiled woman.

Foreigners rarely stay here. The city is polluted. Unromantic. The few Westerners I have met have told me this. Many pass through by train en route to better-known places: Sichuan Province to the north and, to the south, Yunnan. When your work is over, you will step out of our lives, and after you have left, you will begin to see me, as I now see Mrs F, from a great distance, a waning memory.

The memory is already waning as the Little Gentleman farewells me at the bus stop. Evening is falling, casting a veil over the valley.

The bus competes with horse-drawn carts, cars and bicycles. The skies emulate the dark hues of the Renoir, while the evening light intensifies the dreamlike quality of the landscape.

When I arrive back in Huaxi I am reluctant to return to the apartment. I make my way to the riverbank. There is a chill in the air. The winter is long over, but the cold lingers. The fields are in darkness and the bridge is deserted. The first stars are out, and through the doorway of the mill I see a single globe and, beneath it, the miller seated on his stool, pipe in hand, deep in reverie.

I step inside. The mill is enclosed by farmland and limestone ranges, lost in a dream of the Middle Kingdom. I have come through the mountains and am enveloped by them. In this moment, this is my reality. All that exists is a room lit by a single globe, the miller seated beside me. And the *thoom, thoom, thoom* of the wheel, an endless churning.

I return at dawn, and cross the river shallows on a series of stones to the pavilion, upstream from the watermill. It has been my habit to come here at this hour to escape the martial music and the strident homilies and slogans that boom from the college speakers every morning.

On one side of the pavilion are fields and ascending paddies. On the other are parklands and, on the horizon, the familiar outline of the mountains. Some fifty metres downstream the river flows over an outcrop of rocks and quickens into rapids. On weekends art students line the banks with their easels. They paint in oils, working layers of blues and silvers to capture the textures of the cascading waters.

And he is there, as he is most mornings. The old man is walking with steady steps along the bank in the park opposite the pavilion, carrying a bamboo birdcage covered in a blue cloth. He stops at a tree, places the cage on the ground, takes off his flannel jacket and hangs it on the lowest branch. He bends over, removes the cloth from the cage and suspends it on the branch, beside the jacket.

The songbird begins to sing as soon as the cloth is lifted. For half an hour, the old man performs tai chi beneath the tree. He faces east, to catch the first rays of the sun. There are other people in the park practising their chosen form—each within their private sphere of intimacy. For some it's tai chi, for others chi gong. Younger men and women are performing martial arts.

A woman dressed in a black flannel jacket, white runners and loose-fitting black trousers shadow boxes. Her hair is kept in place by a blue headband. She is stocky in build, but lithe in movement. She assumes a succession of postures and delivers blows with lightning swiftness. She lifts the scimitar she had placed on the grass beside her, parries and thrusts, pirouettes and lunges at her imagined opponent.

A young man practises Kung-Fu monkey style. He moves on tiptoe; his body is loose and his arms are bent at the elbows. He raises them to his face and droops his wrists like monkey paws. He drops on all fours and leaps back upright. His head jerks from side to side, and his eyes dart about, alert and curious, like a watchful monkey. Then, without warning, he lunges forward, fingers clawed, and cuts loose with a flurry of kicks and jabs.

Another man performs drunk-boxing style. He lurches and falls on his back, feigning drunkenness. He moves as if unbalanced, and wobbles and parries to avoid imagined blows. Suddenly, his body is tensed, then triggered into action. The jerking legs and hands are transformed from helplessness into lethal weapons. The abrupt change disarms his opponent. It is an ancient strategy.

The old man takes the same route every morning. He stops at the same tree, hangs the cage and jacket on the same branch and performs the same sequence of movements. He has never shown any sign that he knows I am watching; and I have never tried to speak to him.

He may have been a teacher, a scholar. Perhaps a retired engineer or a party functionary, perhaps a farmer. It does not matter. I am drawn to his serenity and composure. He lives outside and beyond time. I cannot imagine who he had once been, where he received his training, nor what he has witnessed, and this is how I prefer it.

He is there even on mornings when rain threatens. When it falls, the stepping-stones are submerged, forcing me to pick my way with great care to the pavilion. The water swirls at my feet and tumbles over the rocks, finding new pathways between them. Crabs scuttle to higher ground. The earth is pungent with damp. Water pours down the shingled roof and slides down the lacquered poles of the pavilion.

The old man appears on time, cage in hand, wearing a rain-cape. The cloth on the cage is covered by a sheet of plastic. In his other hand, he holds an umbrella. He stops beneath the tree, hangs the birdcage on the lowest branch, and suspends the open umbrella beside it. It provides a dry space where he can perform his movements. The limestone peaks are shrouded in cloud, and the birdsong is drowned out by the rush of the water. But it remains a part of the soundscape: a presence. The bird does not sing in vain.

Soon others appear—children on their way to school and workers taking shortcuts to the town, stepping warily over the stones under their capes and umbrellas. Two young boys stand on the muddy banks and launch branches into the river. They watch them until they disappear over the rapids.

And all the while the old man continues his practice. His feet are firmly grounded, his body erect but supple, his hands and arms flowing. He follows his routine at the same unhurried pace. Once done, he covers the cage and retrieves the umbrella. Within minutes he is gone into the rain and cloud: Han Shan, vanishing towards Cold Mountain.

The Spring Festival is long over, but the turning of the seasons has stalled. For weeks, the skies are covered in cloud; people scurry to and from work beneath the steady rainfall. Winter has reclaimed residence, but still I walk every afternoon and, at times, at dawn and nightfall.

And still they come to my apartment, my students, to tell their stories. In turn, I visit them in their spartan rooms, composed of single beds on concrete floors and cane chairs at tables piled with books and papers. On the walls, perhaps a map of Guizhou or a poster of a Chinese film star. And I visit those higher in status, the older lecturers, the party cadres and their families, in their modest quarters.

Take for instance the Beijing Man. He is a culinary magician. The tiny balcony of his flat is his kitchen, and from a small gas stove he produces gourmet dishes: hot and sour soup, stir-fried egg and tomato, fish cooked with five-spice powder, and fried tofu with egg wrapping. He steps back into the living room and delivers the dishes to the table. After the meal is done, we shift the table against the wall along with the chairs and sofa. He switches on a cassette recorder and plays a medley of tangos.

The Beijing Man is a teacher of Russian and English. He conducts the college orchestra in his arrangements of Western classics. Beethoven. Mozart. Tchaikovsky. He can be found, on any night, at one of the dance parties that break out in the college, where students practise steps—ballroom and, increasingly, disco—that were until recently off limits and which are still frowned on by old-school cadres.

The Beijing Man dresses in style. In winter, he wears a dark wool coat, in summer, open-necked shirts and flannel jackets. At fifty, his hair is dyed black and is slicked back from his forehead. He wears a tan suit and a tan tie on a white shirt, freshly ironed. He guides his partner to the cassette music, on the diagonal, making maximum use of the space available. He twirls her round with a theatrical flourish and glides back on the return journey. There is a lightness in his step, a playfulness in his movements, and on his face, a smile of exuberance.

He stops mid-step, mid-dance, abruptly. I have seen this before, this sudden change in mood. He slumps back in a chair.

His youthful complexion gives way to creases and furrows. The mischievous smile and the good cheer are gone, replaced by a plaintiff moaning.

I cannot wait until I'm allowed to leave Guizhou, he says. He is a city boy. The fields hold little attraction for him, and the landscape no romance. All he sees is the dirt and impoverishment. There is something else that goads him and drives his mood shifts. It can be triggered by the thought of what could have been. He cannot overcome his sense of a life betrayed, and of the best years of his life wasted here in Huaxi, Guizhou Province, the place of his exile.

There is one fragment of landscape, a specific stretch of road that skirts the fields overlooked by the college. When he sees it, his rage wells up. He is overcome by nausea. He quickens his steps when he has no choice but to take it. The mountains appear mute, as they did when he was being paraded from the college.

The mob was at his back. His students and colleagues were his accusers. He was bent over and crouched like a dog. Whenever he lifted himself from the crouch, he was pushed back down. You are a dog, so you must walk like a dog, the mob shouted, and he resumed his dog-crawl shuffle along the road where I now set out on my daily walks into the countryside.

It began in 1957, he says. He was a student at the Beijing Foreign Languages Institute, active in college theatre, an actor, singer and dancer. He performed excerpts from Beijing opera. He loved harmony and form, movement and rhythm. He was having the time of his life.

'Let a hundred flowers blossom and a hundred schools of

thought contend,' urged Mao. You are free to criticise the party. If you criticise the party, you will be loved by the party. The Beijing Man had no interest in politics, but he couldn't resist the Siren's call. He was in his early twenties, naive, he will say, years later. If he takes part in the movement, he reasoned, it will increase his popularity among fellow students and his esteem in the eyes of party leaders. And the slogan appealed to him; he was beguiled by its poetry.

He took part in political meetings. He stood at the microphone and addressed mass audiences. He denounced the party-controlled press. It reports only good news, he said, never the bad. He called for free speech and extolled the virtues of creativity. He was cheered and encouraged. He adored the spotlight.

Mao changed course. Those who criticised the party had revealed themselves. The Beijing Man was outed as a 'rightist'. He was separated from his fellow students and was no longer allowed to take part in activities. Fellow rightists were sent to prison camps or to the countryside to be re-educated. A close friend committed suicide. She could not accept her fall from grace, the humiliation.

The Beijing Man graduated in 1960 and was exiled to Guizhou Province. He was assigned to the agricultural college as a teacher of Russian. After arriving in Huaxi, he wept every day for months. He could not stand the dusty streets and the coarseness of provincial life.

He stood in a classroom each week, harangued by teachers and students. For hours on end they accused him, called him a counter-revolutionary, a running dog of Imperialism. In his language classes there were students assigned to report on him. Out of class no one dared speak to him. He could not reveal his feelings or display any weakness. It would have confirmed his 'bourgeois' tendencies.

He fell in love with a nurse who worked in a local hospital. They were told by the leaders that they could not marry. Her father lived in Nanjing. He was a high-ranking party official. The party secretary at the hospital reported on their relationship. Her father was enraged.

On the eve of the wedding, the Beijing Man made his way to the hospital to collect his fiancée's belongings. He intended to shift them to his room in the college, where they were to begin married life, but her room had been stripped of furniture, clothes and bedding. There was no trace of her. She had left Huaxi, the hospital administrator told him. She was at Guiyang Station, heading for Nanjing, returning to her family. There was nothing he could do about it.

The Beijing Man dashed outside. He ran frantically through the streets in search of transport. He climbed onto the back of a truck headed for Guiyang; he held onto the jolting tray, but he could not hold onto his sanity. He made out the black outlines of the ranges. The countryside dark and forbidding. Time was running out. The mountains were outpacing him. The lights of Guiyang were on the horizon, close but receding.

When the truck pulled up at the station, he jumped from the tray and dashed like a madman for the entrance. He careered between passengers. His face was hot and his temples were beating. He found his fiancée on the platform. The train was waiting. He sprinted towards her. She was within reach, but the platform was shaking; his feet buckled and gave way beneath him. He was falling. His hands reached out for the concrete. When he woke, he was lying on the ground and she was bending over him.

Why, he asked her? Why? She was silent. Why? No one knew why any longer. It was a word no one dared utter in public. Why? She was forbidden to tell him. He was beyond caring, or knowing. There were forces beyond his control. She had been ordered to see her father, she said. She had to go to Nanjing. I will come back, she said. I promise.

The Beijing Man returned to the college. For weeks, he was feverish. He couldn't sleep and he couldn't concentrate. His fiancée remained in Nanjing. Her father took her aside every day. It would be an insult to the family for her to marry a counter-revolutionary, he said. What he had achieved would be dishonoured, his laborious rise through the ranks in the party, for nothing.

I have risked my life for the people, he berated her. If you marry him, the family will lose face. You will take us down with you. She changed her mind from day to day, bent to his wishes, then recanted, then submitted again. That was how it went. The days became weeks and still her father harangued her.

The college president wrote that the Beijing Man was ill. The letter jolted her from her uncertainty. She had to return, she said. She had made up her mind. If you do this you will no longer be my daughter, her father told her. He bent down, drew an imaginary line on the floor, and said: You are on the right, and I am on the left. If you don't cross back over, I will disown you. His daughter returned to Huaxi, to the Beijing Man. Her father did not speak to her for twenty years.

The following year their first daughter was born, but the struggle was not over. All teachers were required to live in the college. Every day, from dawn until late at night, slogans blared from loudspeakers to a backdrop of martial music, and three times a day, at the appointed hour, the Beijing Man stood in front of the students and staff, wearing a dunce's hat.

He had to say 'yes' to every accusation. Yes, I am guilty. Yes, I am a dog, a reactionary. He stood in front of a portrait of Mao, red book in hand, and repeated: I am sorry. I am not a good man. I ask Chairman Mao for forgiveness.

His first daughter had a high fever. He ran to the hospital room where she was with her mother. When he took his daughter in his arms, a Red Guard seized her from him. You are not allowed to talk to the new generation, he said. You will corrupt your daughter. The cadre dropped the infant on the bed. He did not allow the Beijing Man to touch her.

The Beijing Man fled the hospital and took the path to the river. The mountains were menacing sentinels. The taunts of the Red Guard haunted him. He ran to the bridge, stood by the edge and stared at the water. He imagined himself embraced in its coolness.

A second daughter was born. When she took ill, he rushed to her room in the hospital. His wife was on nursing duty. He opened the door and saw his first daughter, now four years old, kneeling on the ground, tending her baby sister. The sight terrified him. Again, he had been prevented from being a father. Again, he made his way to the bridge, and again he thought of surrendering to the river.

He was ordered to labour on the college farm. He worked from dawn till dusk, and returned home each night exhausted. This is how it was for a decade, until 1976 and the death of Mao. The following year the central government allowed criticism of the suffering that had occurred, and proclaimed they had been in error. The Beijing Man was exonerated and permitted to resume his vocation.

There is supper on the table: sweet dumplings, glutinous rice cakes, candied fruit and chocolate. The Beijing Man sees none of it. On his face is an expression of sullen anger. They asked you to criticise them, and then they punished you, he says. The injustice still rankles.

He looks about him, as if suddenly remembering his surroundings. He runs a hand across his forehead, straightens his back and assumes his upright posture. His eyes regain focus. His face brightens, and his playful smile returns.

This, I suspect, is how it will always be, the Beijing Man fluctuating between a childlike sense of mischief and his outrage. He has no interest in taming this. It is who he is, and what history has made of him. Take it or leave it. He reaches for the cassette player and switches it back on. He is still dancing when I leave the apartment.

~

Again, I am not ready to return home. I take the route to the river, the same path that the Beijing Man took in the times of his anguish, contemplating suicide. Many did take their own lives. The Beijing Man was sustained, he says, by his two daughters. He could not forsake them. They pulled him back from the brink.

The fields are quiet, the farmers lost in the sleep of the exhausted. Their days are spent transplanting rice seedlings. They will be back in the fields at dawn, backs bent in the cool of sunrise. The watermill is at rest. The lights are out and the brick structure is shrouded in darkness.

I walk beyond the bridge to the water's edge, to a clearing with a clear view of the mill and, upstream, the waterfall, and further still, the pavilion. I have sat here often, marking my students' work. I have stopped here several times with N when he accompanied me on my walks.

Han Shan and William Blake are similar in spirit, says N, seated beside me in the clearing one afternoon. He takes a book from his shoulder bag, a volume of English poetry. They worshipped nature and wanted to be at one with it. It is said that Han Shan, when pursued by officials, slipped through a crevice that closed behind him and was never seen again. He vanished when the authorities tried to evict him. Others say he vanished when fleeing a group of men delivering clothes and medicines.

He did not welcome their assistance. 'Thieves,' he cried out as they approached. And just as they reached out to grab him, he was gone, through the crack. The fissure disappeared and was replaced by a smooth surface. Others say he leapt into a cave that closed after him. Some say that he was a buffoon and a lunatic.

Some believe his spirit resides in the mountain. There are those who believe he is the mountain.

N chuckles. He reads me a line from Blake: 'Improvement makes straight roads; but the crooked roads without improvement are roads of genius.' Days later, he presents me with Blake's words on a sheet of red paper, in both Chinese characters and in English, written with typical care over the calligraphy.

It is the same care that N would apply to the translation of the couplet the miller had asked me to write weeks before I was due to leave the province. A couplet is a complex undertaking N had told me. The lines must match each other in the number of characters. The tones in one line complement the tones in the other. The heading is important too. It integrates the lines and creates a unity.

There are many rules, N said, but don't worry about them. You are working in English. The meaning of what you write is more important. Your task is to depict the essence of what you have experienced here.

Yet, how to write it? How to evoke in two lines the many paths, both straight and crooked, I have walked; the tales that have come my way and the images that flood my mind when I sit down to the task in my apartment.

Of the travelling magician who stopped in Huaxi on market days, erecting a makeshift stage beneath a tarpaulin supported by bamboo poles and a patchwork of materials, who had then bounded on stage, wearing a shabby grey suit and a red tie over a white shirt, repeating his show, hour after hour, while audiences huddled under umbrellas to shield themselves from the rain leaking into the shelter. He performed in a rasping voice and a non-stop patter interspersed with mime, drawing belly laughs. He made coins rain from all corners of the stage into a top hat, and made watches appear and vanish. He disgorged unbroken chains of paper from his mouth, and twisted pieces of string into spaghetti. He transformed pieces of cloth into rows of flags and, with a snap of his fingers, set them fluttering. He cast a spell over the crowd, building anticipation, readying them for the appearance of his reptiles.

With a trumpet fanfare from his female assistant, he opened a wooden box that had sat all the while on a pedestal. He enticed a cast of cobras from it, prodded and kissed them, and then returned them to the box and conjured a python, three-metres in length, which he wound around his assistant as she lay stretched out on a table. Then he reopened the box, released the cobras, and arranged them in a writhing circle around the python-bound woman: the grand finale.

And how to convey what I had observed on bus trips to the outlying villages, where I followed remote paths to hamlets tucked in the folds of mountain ranges and trekked through passes squeezed between cliffs like an afterthought—coming across valleys sunk in stillness, from which there rose the bellowing of a bullock and the voice of a woman singing a melody of the hill tribes.

Towards evening, I had sat on the lower slopes awaiting the bus to Huaxi. The sun descended behind the village, closing the gap of light between sky and horizon. Clothes fluttered on lines strung across the alleys behind me: navy blues, mauves and whites against the ochres of mudbrick houses. Clay paths climbed from the valley, along which people were making their way home from the Sunday market.

Women walked with rattan coups on their backs and cackling hens strapped alongside babies. A farmer drove a herd of cows with a sharp-eyed hawk perched on his shoulder. A group of shoemakers carted boxes packed with glues, wooden lasts and slabs of leather. A posse of men rode packhorses, weighed down with merchandise. Cyclists struggled up inclines with ducks strapped to the handlebars.

And still they came: on tractors, engines stuttering under their loads of goods and passengers. On trucks and horse-drawn carts, wheels wobbling and creaking, drivers whipping their fatigued horses when they slackened. A file of men carried wooden bed frames, steadying them with their raised arms, while holding them aloft like barbells. Old men, pipes in their mouths, laboured under bundles of timber alongside a younger man with a wooden plough on his shoulder. A girl with a load of hay twice her size strung on her back, walked behind a group of youths clustered around a blaring ghetto-blaster. Men and women balanced cages of squealing piglets on bamboo rods, jogging to sustain the momentum.

Despite the weight and the fatigue there was a sense of lightness and festivity. The day was done and the haggling was over. The deals had been sealed, the goods bartered. And they were approaching their homes, the bus groaning up the bitumen roadway—its tyres flattened under the cargo of passengers and the luggage strapped to the roof, stuffed under seats and squashed in the aisles to double as seating.

The sky swelled with black clouds in the final moments of daylight. I boarded the bus and clung to a strap inside the doorway, and rocked with the weary bodies crowded around me. A burst of rain caught the driver unawares and blocked his vision. In the seconds before he turned on the lights, the bus was suspended in darkness. The mountains turned black. All sign of outside movement ceased and the valley vanished. A streak of lightning revealed pools glistening in roadside ditches, and the file of men, women and children, strung out as far as the eye could see, returning from market.

And how to encompass the stone carver lost in his dream of dragons and serpents; and the Little Gentleman leading me with bold steps through the *hutongs* of Guiyang city; and my students, seated six days a week, four hours each morning in the classroom—many of whom had recounted their life stories, their regrets and aspirations and taken me with them to their hometowns and hamlets.

And strolling home, in the early hours, after social gatherings with Mr M the language teacher: rotund, jocular and short, approaching fifty, and seemingly content with his lot, taking in extra students for private tuition, getting rich. Well, let's call it rich relatively speaking, he'd said, with a sardonic smile—enough cash for a TV and trips to Yunnan and the Stone Forest. Enjoy yourself, he'd said. You never know how long it will last.

A friend of his leant out of a second-floor apartment window and invited him up for a game of chess. Mr M took his leave and, like an excited child, darted through the doorway and up the steps. The men's shadows fell on the curtain. They were still playing when I passed by at sunrise.

And how to portray the farmer bent over double, transplanting rice seedlings in a flooded paddy. Briefly stopping, unwinding her supple spine, hands on hips, her dirt-encrusted feet firmly planted. Looking up from beneath her conical hat at the mountain ranges, holding her gaze for a moment, then bending back, vertebra by vertebra, with the elasticity of the branches of a weeping willow, to resume her relentless labour.

And how to convey my friendship with the old boatman of Baihua-Hu, One Hundred Flower Lake, a thirty-minute drive from Huaxi. The boatman rowed me from a small landing. He stood at the stern, gripping two crossed oars, while rocking back and forth to the rhythm. Behind him, mountain peaks and forested slopes tumbled down to banks strewn with wildflowers and willows.

The boatman lives on the lake. He is a Buyi man, and the Buyi worship water. And on water, the boatman is at ease, even as he rows against gathering storms and sharp breezes. He ferries me to the middle of the lake, to his home island. We scramble up the banks to a hamlet of wooden houses.

On land, the boatman is a wiry gnome, running about, tending to chores, chatting. He tells of famines, when the villagers lived on roots and leaves, and the stems of wild plants and flowers. Seventy years ago, massive floods forced his family off the land. They took refuge on the hilly island and subsisted on fish and rice and a meagre income derived from rape oil.

The walls of the central room are insulated with newspaper, on which there hang Spring Festival posters and photos of the boatman and me, taken on previous visits. The floor is clay, the furniture basic: several wooden stools and a table. His grandchild, a boy of five, sits on a stool beside him. We eat egg soup, soya beans and vegetables for lunch, washed down with white wine and spirits.

Back on the water, he points out features of the lake and the surrounding landscape. The boatman views the world with a child's rapt attention. The features have stories to tell, and he is their interpreter. He releases a hand from one of the oars and points. Look. Look. That vertical rock jutting out of the lake is a candle to heaven. Look. The larger rock in the middle of the lake is the general, and the rocks strewn around him are his soldiers awaiting orders to charge into battle.

Look. That rock is known as the monkey, and those rolling hills are a flock of swallows. If you look carefully, you can see they are about to take flight. Look, and you will see them move, just a fraction. He holds his thumb and forefinger close, and rocks the boat with unrestrained laughter, then sings ballads of ill-fated lovers: *Even a good horse cannot go any faster to Beijing/ Even competent officials cannot help a family in trouble/ And even the most devoted of parents cannot help their children in their love problems.*

It is late afternoon. The boatman's strokes are precise and even. The oars slice the water, leaving barely a ripple. An egret stands motionless on a rock pillar. Wild ducks take flight, and their shadows form black streaks on the lake's surface. A flock of gulls pass overhead, wings gilded by the setting sunlight. A farmer, carrying a mattock, descends a narrow path, making his way home from his farmlands.

The boatman falls silent. He scans the waters about him. He lengthens his strokes, then allows the boat to glide on its own momentum. The first stars are appearing; a crescent moon is rising; the islets and rocks are jagged outlines. The boatman knows I do not want it to end, that I crave more time to take it in; he takes a circuitous route back to the landing.

The boatman is the vital force in the setting. Without him the lake would be stagnant. He carries the smell of earth, water and labour. He watches over the lake, and watches over me. He instils confidence. He is there, in the darkness, after I am gone, rowing back home to his island; and his presence remains with me now, long after I have returned to my apartment.

And how to encompass that Sunday walk, on a winter's day, climbing above the city of Guiyang on East Mountain, past the last factory, and the last of the back-of-the-truck Sunday markets. The vehicles gathered in a vacant lot, and the goods laid out on blankets and makeshift tables—pyramids of noodles, eels writhing in buckets, hessian sacks overflowing with red kidney beans.

The muddied path ascended beyond the commerce and busy-ness. The crowd milled outside a house on a hillside hamlet. I was invited into a tree-lined courtyard. Upwards of twenty people were bent over woks, cooking rice, pork and vegetables. Bouquets of flowers and wreaths were lined up against the walls, and white pennants hung from the upper branches.

A group of women tended an altar on a coffin, made up of candles and incense, paper cut-outs of male and female figures and offerings of food in dishes laid out in front of the photo of an elderly man—the latest inductee into the gallery of ancestors. I was a guest at a Taoist funeral, ushered inside the house and given a seat beside members of the deceased's family. Women sat with babies in their arms, and infants crawled on the tiled floor. Visitors filed in and out to pay their respects, their voices reduced to a murmur.

The men and women sat separately. The bereaved relatives wore white cloths wound into turbans. A hum of subdued chatter was interrupted by the cries of the dead man's son, triggering the weeping of fellow mourners. Their cries rose in a shrill chorus, then withdrew into an unnerving stillness, broken when the food was carried in from the courtyard. The mood abruptly shifted from mourning to exuberance. The wine and spirits were flowing, and we stood, arms on each other's shoulders, singing.

I continued my climb, behind horse-drawn carts loaded with sand and boulders. The horses laboured up a clay path that led to a Taoist temple. Beside the gateway stood a two-roomed cottage. I was invited inside, as if expected, by two men in ankle-length blue gowns.

The older man, in his eighties, warmed his hands by a coal stove that sat between two beds, while the other, a man in his forties, stood in the adjoining room, stirring the evening meal on a wood stove. His grey-black tresses were tied in a bun, and his gown hugged his plump figure. He brought a kettle to the boil, and served tea. We sat beside the wood stove. Outside, a winter's day, and inside the three of us drinking quietly.

I moved on from the gatekeepers' cottage. The narrowing path wound to a pagoda-style temple. Carpenters were at work on the veranda, restoring the lattice work, replacing window frames where the old ones had rotted. I climbed beyond the temple on a stone path built into the cliff face.

The ascent was made only slightly less dangerous by a guardrail still in the process of being erected. Labourers hauled rocks from the carts and delivered them to the stonemasons. The exhausted horses, heads bowed, stood silently, released from their burden. The masons squatted on the path, carving out steps to restore those worn down by the feet of countless pilgrims.

The steps petered out at a giant Buddha sculpted in the rockface. The statue was riddled with chinks where it had been stoned, a decade earlier, by mobs of Red Guards in a wild fury. The mountain was alive with work: the sawing of wood, and the clinking of metal on stone. Gathering clouds hung like a shroud over the city below. Standing beside the Buddha and the masons at work on its restoration, I sensed that which outlives the rise and fall of dynasties, counterpointed by the stillness of this moment.

How to convey all this? And the many routes I had followed in the valley, the farmers plying me with drink, then leaving me to make my way on crooked paths that inevitably led me to the stone bridge, the river. The willow and the mill taking shape, the tiled roof coming into focus.

Then, through the open doorway, the sight of the miller

going about his work, a dependable presence, and, minutes later, the singing of the kettle, the deliberate movements as he poured the water into the teapot. And the two of us—the foreigner and the miller—seated side by side, cups in hand, engaged in wordless conversation.

The heading of the couplet was obvious: *Huaxi Watermill.* As for the two sentences, the task seemed impossible. How could I emulate, in English, the classical Chinese form: the three, five or seven characters that each line was composed of? These were conventions, said M, that even the anarchic Han Shan followed.

I chose to concentrate, as he had advised, on the meaning. I deliberated over each line, and considered alternatives. I weighed each word. Crossed out. Rephrased. Rearranged the order, adding and subtracting, retrieving and rejecting, backtracking, then moving forward.

I focused on the letters, as they physically took shape, with the care I had observed when Q translated his father's final testament and the care I had seen taken by market calligraphers, writing letters and statements on behalf of semi-literate farmers; and as I had noted in the deliberate way that the miller had entered the names and amounts of grain delivered by the farmers into his ledger.

And I saw the limits of words, of language as a futile attempt to encapsulate lived experience, and doomed to a kind of failure. I wanted to convey the detached warmth of the miller and his acceptance of my presence, and to do justice to the tales I have recounted here, and those that will remain untold, for that's how it is with all journeys.

I paused over one word—in the second line of the couplet—for a long time. I could not decide between 'mind' and 'heart'. Finally, I wrote the couplet, taming my untidy script, acutely aware that this is a country where the handwriting itself is an integral part of the content.

N lays out the Four Treasures: the inkstick, the brushes, the paper and the inkstand. He adds water to the bowl carved into the inkstand, and stirs the inkstick in a circular motion. It is his parting gift, a demonstration of the Four Treasures in action. The inkstick dissolves in the water. He tests the texture and consistency, and when he is satisfied, he chooses a brush, dips it in and applies the brush to the red paper.

Each stroke is an act of control and focus. In his calm approach to his work and the firmness of his strokes N personifies the qualities his grandmother wished for him—to be kind but strong, at ease, yet disciplined. Hand and mind in equilibrium. Each stroke glistens for a moment, then is absorbed by the paper.

At this point, there is no turning back, says N. Each brushstroke is spontaneous, but once painted it is permanent. It cannot be duplicated; the calligrapher's current mental state is captured and fixed on paper. I am reminded of the testament penned by Q's father on the eve of his death, the sense of urgency he must have felt as he applied each brushstroke, and his battle to steady his shaking hands, taming them one last time into submission.

Each stroke, says N, must be applied in the prescribed

order. He paints the characters representing *Huaxi Watermill* horizontally. *Hua* meaning flower, *xi* meaning stream: hence flower-stream. The couplet poses a greater challenge. N takes time over the translation, seeking characters that will best convey the meaning of the original.

He paints the first vertical line. People reading it, he says, will imagine different landscapes. They will see their hometowns and the places they have travelled. They will be reminded of their times of exile, and their partings and reunions. They will see the alternative paths, the chance encounters, and the life choices that have led them here.

He paints the second vertical line. The two lines are in conversation, N says. They conduct a dialogue, which will begin when the words are in place by the doorway. There will be people passing by, he says, who will stop to contemplate each character and bring their own interpretation. Some will step in close and inspect each stroke with a critical eye. Others will step back to view the entire scene: the heading, the vertical lines, then the mill, and the mountains—the backdrop as a living canvas.

Calligraphy is the highest artform, N says, and each line is suggestive of many meanings. When he paints the character for *mind*, he tells me that my debate over this word had found its own solution. In Mandarin, he says, there is a character for mind and heart that can be read as one and the same.

~

We take the completed banners to the mill, unfurl them by the doorway, and work with the miller to glue them into place. Then we step back and survey our work, making sure the vertical lines on either side of the door are of the same height, and the heading centred above the lintel. When we are done, the miller pours the tea. The two lines by the door have begun their conversation.

We sit, side by side, and observe the contours of the limestone ranges, the tableau contained by the open doorway. They are as reassuring in their familiarity as the scenes that may have greeted Han Shan from his retreat on the heights of Cold Mountain. We sit on wooden stools, drinking quietly. And beneath us, the waterwheel: *Thoom. Thoom. Thoom.* Round and round, an endless churning.

I come from a distant place to Huaxi Watermill.
Here I feel at peace; my mind becomes still.

The Ballad of Keo Narom

I met Keo Narom in Phnom Penh on 26 January 2013 at a workshop I conducted for Cambodian writers. She approached me during the afternoon break. She had a story she wished to tell me, she said, and handed me her card: 'Keo Narom, PhD. Researcher and book writer for children' printed in Khmer and English.

We had little time to talk during that first meeting, but Narom did not appear hurried. She was composed and quietly spoken. She talked of the deaths of her husband, her father, her brothers and sisters and her four children during the Khmer Rouge era. A younger sister survived. *Ma petite soeur,* Narom says with affection. It was, she would later tell me, the first time she had begun to recount her story. After all, she had to find a way to get on with life.

The grief will never be overcome. How can it be? Narom does not allow herself to dwell too long on her lost ones lest the ghosts return to haunt her. *En avance*, she says as we return to the workshop. Always forward.

A full moon night. The dogs are barking. They interrupt my sleep as they do most evenings. The barking begins across the road from my hotel room at the late-night eatery that is a pit stop for tuk-tuk drivers and nightshift workers. A black mutt sprawls by the entrance.

The night arouses its fury. One shrill bark begets another, stretching to the far reaches of the city. Each bark cuts deeper into my sleep until I am fully awake. Outside, five floors down, dogs are conducting a long-distance argument, while in the eatery the customers are engaged in post-midnight conversation.

At dawn the dogs are at it again. I give up, get dressed, take the lift to the lobby and set out on the half-hour walk to the Tonle Sap River. The streets are lined with garlanded portraits of Prince Norodom Sihanouk. His body lies in state in the royal palace, as it has since his death in Beijing the previous October. Sticks of incense burn on street altars set up in his honour. His cremation is to take place in two weeks, in a purpose-built stupa.

People are out walking and exercising. Groups of bare-chested men play kick-shuttlecock. The shuttles hurtle over the nets at great speed; the players' skills are breathtaking. Entire families are camped on the streets. Some lie in hammocks slung between trees on the footpaths. Others go about their morning ablutions. Pilgrims file across the royal forecourt to lay flowers at Sihanouk's state altar; the chants of Buddhist monks ring out over a loudspeaker.

I have come full circle. When I was last here, in January 1970, Sihanouk was in power and war was raging in Vietnam alongside a secret war to the north, in Laos. I had travelled for weeks through both countries. Arriving in Phnom Penh from war-torn Saigon was a relief. Back then, it seemed Cambodia was an enclave of peace, bar the not-so-secret US bombings on the Cambodian–Vietnamese border, ostensibly to destroy Viet Cong hideouts.

Sihanouk appeared to be the undisputed leader—jazz saxophonist, film director, actor, scriptwriter, composer and the founding father of the republic—a dilettante for all seasons, playing off all sides to remain neutral. He presided over a low-rise city graced with Parisian-style boulevards and villas built in the style of its colonial masters.

The peace was deceptive. Forces were building. Foreign powers and their proxies were vying for ascendancy: the US and China jousting in the shadows. Sihanouk was about to be overthrown and the US-backed Lon Nol installed as leader. Civil war was brewing.

I travelled northwest from Phnom Penh to a Cambodian border post, and set out, rucksack on my back, to walk a barren stretch of dirt to the Thai border: No Man's Land. I recall time passing slowly. Each sound was amplified—the faint drone of a truck, the crunch of dirt beneath my feet, each birdcall—alternating with an uneasy silence.

I was exposed, an easy target in the sights of guns trained on me from both sides. As I walked, one stretch of barbed wire was retreating and, in the distance, another approaching. The stillness heightened my sense of fragility, but in an unexpected surge of defiance, I was tempted to stop mid-walk, put down my pack and set up camp within sight of the two borders. The tension eased as I drew close to Thailand, though I felt a sense of disquiet at departing Cambodia, a country where I had felt welcome.

No one, however, could have foreseen the horror about to unfold, the years of murder and terror that were to descend, as this small country was subjected to the fury of contending powers, driving its people into the hands of fanatical ideologues. I could move on. There would be no such option for the people of the country I was leaving.

After that first meeting with Narom I was eager to hear the full story. I seized the opportunity that evening as we were being driven through the streets of Phnom Penh to a writers' gathering. I sat in the back. R, the convener of the workshops, was driving. Narom sat beside him, dressed in a black and grey checked sarong, an orange silk scarf and mauve jacket. Her dyed-black hair was swept back in a blue headband. Her complexion was strikingly youthful for a woman in her seventies.

The streets by the foreshore were gridlocked. Motorbikes wove in and out of the traffic, finding openings within millimetres of the stationary vehicles. Upwards of one million mourners were making their way to the city to pay their last respects to their 'Father-King'.

To our right ran the waters of the Tonle Sap River. Fishing boats and cruisers moved to and from the shoreline. The river was more enticing at night, free of the sight of refuse littering the banks and the midday haze that leached the water of its colour. To our left, the palace blazed with light. The forecourt was crowded with families strolling on a humid evening.

At first Narom spoke in French, as she had during our first conversation hours earlier. But my French was not fluent enough to grasp the nuances. She switched to Khmer, and R interpreted. We inched past the palace towards the cremation stupa. I was grateful for the heavy traffic and the process of translation. They provided time for me to take in what Narom was saying, and to reflect on the enormity of the story she was telling.

Keo Narom's ordeal began when the Khmer Rouge cadres occupied the city on 17 April 1975. They entered Phnom Penh from the north, in black shirts and black trousers, red sashes tied at the waist, sandals carved out of tyres, and red bandanas. They made their way on foot, on the backs of trucks and in requisitioned vehicles, guns strapped to their backs, bullet belts strung around their shoulders: a ragged army of young men and teenagers moving into the city in advance of their leaders.

Sick of five years of civil war, residents lined the streets and greeted them as liberators. Keo Narom and her husband waved from their balcony. Many were surprised at how young the soldiers were and at their air of suspicion and incomprehension. Some noticed a chilling detail. The boy-soldiers were grim-faced. Something about them was beyond reach. They moved with robotic purpose. Despite the welcome and displays of euphoria, their faces were hardened.

The evacuations began immediately. Khmer Rouge cadres bellowed instructions through loudhailers. As a ruse, they warned the residents of impending American bombings and told them they would be allowed back when the danger was over.

There were fifteen family members in Keo Narom's household: her parents, her husband, her four children—two girls, aged ten and eight, two boys, one six, the youngest, one—several of Narom's siblings, and an aunt. They crowded into two cars and took with them supplies of rice, cooking utensils and a change of clothing. And books and knitting needles, as pastimes for their temporary absence.

They eased past men, women and children trudging on foot and crammed into rickshaws and ox-drawn wagons. It was the hottest time of the year. Those walking had umbrellas and *kramas* for protection. Mothers held babies in their arms, boys and girls carried younger siblings on their backs. They pushed carts, prams and barrows loaded with tinned foods, dried fish and bedding and their personal belongings stuffed in cloth bags, cardboard boxes and baskets. Hospital patients, some attached to their drips, were steered in mobile beds and wheelchairs; the sick and disabled were helped along by relatives.

The entire city was on the move, the residents ordered at gunpoint from shops and businesses, schools, hospitals, government buildings, villas and apartments, and the makeshift huts and tents crammed in fringe camps and pavement settlements that had sprung up to accommodate the two million Cambodians who had sought refuge in Phnom Penh during five years of conflict.

Electrical appliances were stripped from stores and offices and hurled into the river. Buildings were ransacked, libraries stripped, homes gutted. Photos, books, scholarly texts, cassette recorders, washing machines and fridges, lingerie, cosmetics, tailored suits and elegant dresses—the trappings of affluence—were thrown out and set alight. The streets glowed with pyres. Dogs and pigs sniffed through the ashes. Hens pecked over dead embers.

The animals did not last long. They were caught and killed

by hungry Khmer Rouge cadres and fleeing residents. Gangs of scavengers scoured the streets in search of loot. Stalled tanks and factory machinery were scattered on the boulevards. Spectacles, seized from their owners, lay crushed on the pavements. Neighbourhoods, full of life just hours earlier, were silent.

The very idea of the city was being eradicated, the social fabric shredded: universities and colleges, nightclubs, houses of culture, market places, tea houses and cafes, temples and pagodas, museums and galleries—the places where people strolled and gathered—were emptied.

Family members lost each other in the chaos. Frantic mothers searched for their infants. Some who stopped to assist a woman in labour or a sick person were shot to keep the evacuating residents moving forward. Those with cars and trucks drove until they ran out of petrol. In the evening the roadsides were lit by camp fires.

The millions out on the roads were to become known as the April 17th people, enemies of the state simply because they were city dwellers, guilty of having an education, possessing soft hands and wearing glasses, or of being engaged in commerce. They were an amorphous mass to be 're-educated' in the countryside.

The killings began in the very first days, in the city and at roadblocks where identities were checked. Those judged to be collaborators with the overturned regime were singled out—politicians, public servants, military personnel—and executed. Cambodia was to be remade overnight as an agrarian utopia. The clock had been set back to year zero.

Narom and her family made their way towards Oudong District. When they ran out of petrol they abandoned one car and transferred their elderly father and the luggage to the other. They pushed the second car onwards and abandoned it when their way was blocked by a damaged bridge. There was no way back and only one way forward, subject to the dictates of Angkar, the 'Organisation', the shadowy entity that made up the leadership.

Narom's father was the first to go. As a former official in the deposed Lon Nol government, he understood what lay ahead. He had resisted leaving the city during the evacuation and had warned his sons and daughters there would be no returning. Sooner or later they will kill me, he said. Why not spare myself the trouble and make it sooner? The sight of dead bodies en route from Phnom Penh confirmed his suspicions.

He refused to eat, and fought off family members who tried to force-feed him. He spat out the cooked rice they managed to squeeze through, and remained deaf to their entreaties. In his view, he was doing them a favour. The rice they would save by not feeding him would enhance their chances of survival. The second to go was Narom's baby son who came down with dysentery. He died in her arms. Then, her elderly aunt, cut down by exhaustion and illness.

I sit in the back seat and listen to Narom and R intently. The windows are closed, and the interior is cooled by air-conditioning. Each of us has a role: teller, interpreter and listener. Story is the currency that unites us, conferring on us a detached intimacy.

The milling crowds appear like a supporting cast in a pantomime.

There are moments that cut deep in the memory, and this is one of them. All the elements are assembled: the story and the enclosed space in which it is being told, the city so close, yet cut off from hearing. The stillness accentuates the melodious flow of Narom's voice, its shifts in energy and the occasional falter.

I register each change in tone and expression, the slight shaking of her head in disbelief that such things had happened. I feel the gravity of what she is recalling, acutely aware of my own voice as it breaks the silences with questions. I am suspicious of that voice, and fearful of reopening old wounds. Fearful of what the telling is doing to the teller. But, also, possessed by a sense of obligation to hear Narom out. I cannot help but pursue the story.

Keo Narom and her family boarded a crowded motorboat making for Kampong Chhnang Province. They travelled by truck to Pursat Province, and by train to Battambang. Day by day they discarded pieces of luggage until all that remained were the clothes on their bodies. They trudged through the forest, Khmer Rouge cadres at their back, until they arrived at their assigned workplaces, somewhere near the Thai border.

They were woken at three in the morning, and they were forced out to the fields for hard labour. They planted, reaped, hauled rocks and dug ditches. They were stripped of agency and dignity, individuality subsumed into a single insane purpose. They were ill-equipped for unrelenting physical work. Their limbs ached, their minds were numb, and their bodies stank with dirt, sweat and panic. They could not believe what had befallen them.

Narom gazed at the birds flying overhead and envied them their freedom. She looked at her wasted body, and the wasted bodies moving to and from work with her. As she ate her bare rations, she dreamt of the food she once ate in Phnom Penh. She drooled over the memory of the rich, aromatic rice-porridge, her favourite. She was one of the 'new people', the inferior class in the new 'classless' order, underlings to the 'base people', or 'old people' as the peasants and villagers were now titled.

The leaders were seldom seen in public. Perhaps, if they were, the people would have noted the irony: the most prominent leaders were educated abroad: their hands were soft, and their bodies unused to physical labour. Some wore glasses. Starvation, humiliation, interrogation and murder was their modus operandi. And constant movement.

The next to succumb was Narom's husband. A scholar who had studied literature in Czechoslovakia and returned with a master's degree, he had the misfortune of having served as a cultural advisor to the previous government. Stripped of the power to protect his children, he was driven to despair. He killed himself by biting through his tongue and choking on it.

Narom was helpless as she watched her fifteen-year-old brother beaten to death by an enraged cadre who accused him of being lazy. There was no time to mourn, no monks to chant prayers for the dead, and no temples in which to conduct a funeral service. What energy Narom had went towards keeping the dwindling family together. One by one, Narom's children and siblings succumbed to illness and hunger. Perhaps the dead were the fortunate ones, she reasoned—at rest. Released from the terror.

I can see Narom's face in the rear-view mirror. She looks straight ahead; the lights of oncoming cars catch the gold rims of her glasses. Her eyes are alternately lit up and returned to shadow. Her hands have a language of their own. Even within the confines of the car they are in motion. Her fingers form mudras, the classical gestures of Khmer dance. An entire culture is concentrated in her hands and their supple movements.

She catches me watching her. She has registered my concern. She turns to the back seat and says: 'Don't worry. I know how to handle it.' Narom speaks with maternal affection. She is reassuring *me*. She returns her gaze to the road ahead, reverts to her neutral expression, and resumes the telling.

When Narom's youngest sister became ill she was ordered to stay in the village. Narom was sent to a distant work area. She was not permitted to take her two remaining children with her. As she laboured, she held their presence in her mind. She existed only for them. If she lost sight of this she would lose her will and, like her husband and father, she would be finished.

Her entire being was pared back to a single purpose, to be reunited with her children. When word reached her that one of her sons was ill, she begged her overseer, a Khmer Rouge soldier, to allow her to return and look after him.

'Are you a doctor?' he asked.

'I am a mother. I have to take care of my child,' she pleaded.

'You are not a doctor, so how can you help him?' he replied.

That was the end of it. Narom was not present when her older son died. He was nine years old.

When her sister regained strength, and returned to work, Narom was allowed back in the village. By then her last child was starving. Much of the rice that the work brigades produced was allocated to farmers and party cadres. The lower orders were expendable and fed barely enough to keep them useful. Narom foraged in the forest for roots and leaves, bamboo shoots, anything that might have been edible.

When her child died in her arms, Narom was consumed by grief. She had been robbed of her curiosity and her passion for knowledge. She did not shed a tear, she tells me. She steeled herself against it. She was one of a growing number driven to the edge of madness by the loss of loved ones, tormented by the thought that they could not protect their children, could not save them.

The Khmer Rouge had a slogan to justify the death of children: 'When you dig up the grass, you must remove even the roots.'

On 7 January 1979, Cambodian troops and their Vietnamese allies regained Phnom Penh. The Khmer Rouge regime had lasted three years, eight months and twenty days; the exact length of time remains engraved in Cambodian memory. It would come to be known as the Pol Pot era; and the network of execution sites across the country, as the Killing Fields.

Marooned in Pursat Province, at first Narom had no

knowledge of the liberation. The Khmer Rouge overlords were retreating west to the jungles that would become their final stronghold. They tried to coerce the people they had enslaved to come with them. They appealed to the Cambodian suspicion of the Vietnamese, warning them that the Vietnamese would torture and kill them.

Narom's fear of the Khmer Rouge had dissolved with the loss of her children. She knew, instinctively, as did others, that they were losing their grip on power. Narom headed in the opposite direction. She began the long trek to Phnom Penh, three hundred kilometres away. Her sister walked with her.

The sisters set out in March. They slept in forest clearings and in vacant huts when monsoon rains threatened. They met up with people they had known in Phnom Penh before the terror. The group grew. They survived on the rice they found in deserted villages. Narom's sister, twelve years younger and toughened by years of labour, hauled bags of rice on her shoulders.

Narom had difficulty keeping up. She was as thin as a famished monkey, so weak she could barely carry a pot of rice. Her sister urged her to walk faster. Narom sat down on the road, exhausted. 'Why are you sitting down?' her sister asked. 'I am just watching the road,' Narom replied. She laughs at the memory.

As they ran out of rice the sisters traded their last possessions: pillboxes filled with wax. The wax had been used to tend itches, heal skin wounds, and as lipstick. It kept the skin moist, and enabled the women to recover a minute sense of femininity. The Khmer Rouge cadres had allowed them to keep the boxes, because they themselves used the wax and prized its healing properties. For the survivors, the boxes had been a brittle link to the time before, talismanic. Handling them, and rubbing in the wax, evoked flashes of how it had once been, before year zero, a stark contrast to the terror they were enduring.

Not all was well back then. Far from it. But there was life and love and the silver ribbon they called the Tonle Sap winding its way to the mother river, the Mekong; the scent of evening breezes, and the sound of voices murmuring on balconies. The rustle of monks' garments, and the whirring of countless bicycles.

Music surged from bars and cafes, crowds gathered at cinemas. The aroma of food issued from street stalls and residents milled at night markets. Chants echoed from pagodas, marking the passage of the day with a trusted regularity; children spilt from the confines of their classrooms into schoolyards, and with them, laughter...And now? The pillboxes were mere objects to be traded.

The entire country was on the move again, alone, and in small bands, armies of the broken returning to the homes they once lived in. Many walked in the opposite direction, heading for refugee camps on the Thai border, calculating, perhaps, it was time to be done with it and put their beloved but haunted country behind them.

Hens found their wings and lifted themselves into the air, propelled by thirst and hunger to search for water and fodder. Withered buffalo lay prostrate. Wild deer, oxen and pigs roamed the countryside. They drank waters trapped in craters gouged into the terrain by the incessant bombings of fields, paddies, roadsides and forest clearings. The landscape was marked by demolished bridges, razed homes and charred pagodas. Shattered Buddhas.

The sisters trudged on. Their feet and legs were scarred and infected by years of walking barefoot and wading in manure. Their bodies were thin from undernourishment, and their complexions darkened by sun exposure. They were of the earth and the forests, and of the dead and the barely living. Reduced to bone and tendon, beaten skin and wasted muscle.

There were times that they felt unexpectedly light, free of all they had ever possessed, like migrating birds returning to once-known pastures. But those times were short-lived, and they were seized anew with panic at the memory of what they had endured, and by unbidden images of their dead loved ones.

All they could do was will themselves on, step by step, one hardened foot in front of the other, faces turned to the rising sun, backs lit by the sunset. Emboldened by the growing herd that moved with them. The sisters arrived in Phnom Penh on 28 June. They adopted the date as their day of liberation.

We have edged past the cremation stupa. The grounds are lit up; onlookers crowd the cyclone fences. Labourers work around the clock to finish the stupa in time for the funeral. The traffic is easing and gaps are opening. R winds down the windows. The sounds of the night enter—the roar of motorcycles, the revving of cars, pop music blaring.

The spell in the car has been broken, and the delicate thread between the three of us severed. The evening heat is enervating. It is a relief to sit back and allow the flow of the city to wash over us: left to our own thoughts. Returned to silence.

The story is incomplete. There are episodes yet to be recounted, and threads to be unravelled. How had Narom regained the will to live? How had she rebuilt her life and become an ethnomusicologist and a writer of children's stories? A doctor of philosophy? How does a person survive such loss? We will meet again when I return from travelling around Cambodia.

R parks outside the restaurant where our writers' gathering is taking place. *En avance*, Narom says, as she steps out onto the pavement. The grief can never leave her, but there is a steely resolve in her spirit. 'Don't worry,' she repeats. 'I know how to handle it.'

Forty-three years ago, in 1970, I found a place: several hundred kilometres northwest, in Siem Reap Province, called Ta Prohm. Of the many recovered temples of the Khmer kingdoms of Angkor, this was the one that drew me. Thick-limbed fig and silk trees leaned over moss-encrusted tiles and crumbling temples. Fat roots curled around walls, boulders and columns.

Time had crafted a new entity composed of living and dead matter. Tree limbs framed doorways and tracked down stairways, reaching deep into cool sanctuaries. Leaves sprouted from rock crevices, and bas relief tableaux peeped from between branches. The archaeologists too were taken by the temple's ghostly beauty and felt compelled to work around it, enabling the complex to remain somewhat as it was when rediscovered.

I spent many hours there, while what I had seen in Vietnam settled. I was overwhelmed by what I had witnessed. There were ten thousand Australian soldiers in Vietnam back then, and upwards of half a million US troops. Twenty-year-old Australians were being conscripted. My name did not come up in the birthday lottery. Instead I had travelled there on a journalist's visa issued by the Vietnamese embassy in Bangkok.

I had hitchhiked northeast through Thailand, and received rides in jeeps driven by allied servicemen seated beside their Thai girlfriends. I rode with Thai truckies in the elevated cabins of road-trains loaded with military equipment. We stopped overnight in towns that serviced US bases—little Americas, created in the image of the occupying army—from which B-52s set out on their bombing sorties.

I crossed the Mekong into Laos. In the countryside, vast tracts of land were scarred with bomb craters: The Era of the Blue Machine, historians have called it, referring to US bombers engaged in a secret war, which all Laotians knew about. I travelled by plane from Vientiane to the southern city of Pakse, and then to Saigon, flying low over blackened forests that had been carpet-bombed. Carpet, evoking images of beauty and comfort, a euphemism for carnage.

Ta Prohm had offered relief, spaces of solitude and a sense of something far more enduring. Forty-three years later, after hearing Keo Narom's story, and the stories of others who had lived through the Khmer Rouge tyranny, I am drawn back there.

The boat from Phnom Penh to Siem Reap is a single-hull steel ferry. The locked cabin windows are smeared with grime; a karaoke DVD is blaring on a television. The space on the tiny steel deck is tight, but blessedly out in the open, with a view of the banks: a slow-moving landscape of elephant grass, sugar palms, hamlets and pagodas.

The calm is disrupted by the booming voice of an ex-marine. He stands in the narrow aisle between the deck and the guardrail with two cameras slung around his shoulders. His monologue rises above the engine.

'God, this place is beautiful,' he shouts.

His voice is loud and abrasive, his monologue a distraction. Passengers lie on the deck, shielding their faces. Their heads rest on rolled up sleeping-bags and luggage. Their legs are curled, knees tucked in, bodies conforming to confined spaces. But the ex-marine is on his feet. He is untroubled by the heat. He points his cameras at the shore and shoots at random.

'I am in the prime of life,' he says. 'Sixty-five years old and never felt better.' A US marine during the era of war and occupation, he has returned to Vietnam and Cambodia for the first time since 1970.

'We were not there on a picnic,' he shouts. 'We were out there hunting with assault rifles, our M16s against their AK47s. We were shit-scared and we were trained killers. We saw our mates being wounded and killed, and it drove us crazy. We were trigger-itchy. We didn't know who was enemy or ally. It was no picnic. We were out there getting killed, and killing.

'I didn't know what to expect when I came back here, scared of what I might find. Freaked out, and afraid of the memories. Been back a month and I've fallen in love with the place. I'm gonna go back home and fix up my affairs. Gonna pass on my concreting business to my son and come back singing. Gonna spend the rest of my life here. Have fun. And teach the locals about concrete.

'I know everything there is to know about concrete. The concrete here is shit. If a typhoon hit, the buildings would fall like matchsticks. Gonna show the locals how to construct buildings that can last forever.'

His voice rises in and out of hearing. The boat bounces on the water. It moves precariously close to motorised sampans and fishing boats. The ex-marine has got the gift of the gab, and an edge of madness.

'Had a great childhood,' he says. 'Grew up on my grandpa's farm in Nebraska. We raised hogs, grew cherry trees, planted corn and soya beans. We brewed our own beer and made our own corn liquor. It slid down your throat smooth and easy. It brought a smile to your face and warmed your innards. We kids worked on the farm, bailing hay. We sat on the backs of tractors and we roamed the property, hordes of grandchildren running wild together. Man, it was beautiful.'

The boat has moved out onto the Tonle Sap Lake; in this season, it's an inland sea, an expanse of pale blues with a hint of mud floors in its shallower areas. The hours are drifting and the sun is moving towards its zenith. The passengers crammed on the deck are dozing, but the ex-marine is still up and talking. His manic energy is unflagging.

I ease myself off the deck, grab hold of the rail, edge my way to his side and introduce myself. The ex-marine's aftershave is stronger than the breeze-born smells of the water. He exudes a bullish strength that belies his age. He is pleased to have an attentive listener.

'You're a writer, eh? I'm gonna become a writer too. Gonna write a book about the people I've been meeting over a beer on the beach in Sihanoukville, at Sharky's Bar. Every night's a party at Sharky's. You meet people from all over, coming for all kinds of reasons, running away from all kinds of miseries.

'You name it, and you'll find it. Screwed-up marriages. Shonky businesses. Shady dealings. Terminal illnesses. People who hate themselves. And boredom—folks so wealthy they don't know what to do with themselves. They fall in love with the place and bury their troubles. The living's cheap and easy. You would not believe the tales they tell you. Yep, there's a book in this, and I'm gonna write it.

'My hobby is women,' he says, switching tack. There's a glint in his eye. 'I love the women here. Back in '70, I hunted with M16s, now I'm making love not war, like those long-haired pot-smokers used to say. We hated them back then, but now I'm a convert, a believer. I've got no quarrel with anyone.

'Had a great time night before last. Spent it with a lovely lady, a bit older than the others, experienced. She knew what she was doing. And I treated her right. I know how to treat a lady.

'She has two kids to support and I gave her a decent tip in the morning. I also gave her the soap from the bathroom. I gave her the shampoos and conditioners. And I gave her the drinks in the fridge. I gave her the snacks and sweets for her children. Mars bars. Chips, cashews, peanuts, tea bags and biscuits. Salt and sugar. I piled in whatever I could and sent her home happy.'

He laughs a loud unrestrained laugh and snaps pictures of a passing fishing canoe. 'I've got one camera on motor drive,' he says. 'Got another in case the battery runs out, and a bag full of lenses. Zoom lenses. Wide-angle lenses. Telephoto lenses. Got lenses comin' out of my backside. I don't want to miss anything. Life passes by, and if you're not quick it gets away from you.

'I've got a dream. I'm gonna build a boat, a beautiful boat with a serpent's head on the prow. *Nagas*—that's what the Cambodians call 'em. Gonna have a naga's head on the prow and a naga's tail trailing behind it, like you see on the walls of the temples. I got a Cambodian friend who knows how to make 'em. We'll fit it out with orange sails, a loud colour. Man, you're gonna notice this boat.

'I'm gonna sail it all over. Gonna live out my dream. I figure I have twenty years left. A good chunk of time. I'm in reasonable shape; got longevity in the genes. My grandparents lived into their nineties. My parents are still alive in their eighties. Yep. I'm quitting everything. Should have done it long ago. Now I'm doing it for real,' he says, 'and no one's stopping me.'

We motor into the mouth of the Siem Reap River. The waters are down. The banks are lined with ramshackle settlements. The boat scrapes the riverbed as it edges towards its anchorage. The ex-marine is not waiting. He is anxious to get on with it. He hoists himself off the boat, scampers up the clay embankment and dashes across the parking lot to where the tuk-tuks and taxis are waiting. He is out on his own, a tough, nuggetty bastard in shorts, singlet and workboots. A go-getter, pot belly offset by thick thighs and calves, sprinting ahead of the pack, rucksack bobbing on his back. He disappears in the throng; it is the last I see of him.

It's only later, when I examine a map, that I realise that the boat journey, and its route to Siem Reap, has essentially followed the route Keo Narom and her family were ordered out on, northwest, on a brutal journey to slavery: from Phnom Penh via Oudong District to Kampong Chhnang, and from Pursat Province to Battambang.

What had occupied more than three years of horror, I have traversed on a parallel route in a five-hour boat trip, accompanied by the soundtrack of an ex-GI in search of Shangri-la and impoverished women to boost his ageing virility.

It is mid-afternoon when I reach my hotel. I leave my bag in the foyer. Angkor Wat, the main temple, is still open. If I leave now, I can make it. Tourists are heading there to catch the sunset. On the highway, a flotilla of buses, cars, motorcycles and tuk-tuks is travelling in the same direction. Thousands queue at the massive way-stop for tickets, then head back to the highway to rejoin the procession.

I detour to Ta Prohm and get there just before closing time. A band of seven landmine amputees, seated on a wooden platform, play zithers and flutes, two-stringed fiddles, gongs and percussion. Their crutches and prosthetic limbs are stacked against the platform, and their CDs are lined up in front of them. A silver urn sits on a stool, for takings and offerings.

The men play to the chatter of bats and the trill of cicadas. The music blends with the melody of the surrounding forest.

The shadows are lengthening, and the air is thick with the scents of a tropical night. The temple appears as it was when I was last here over four decades ago, tree and rock embracing. It is a homecoming.

I make my way to the main temple of Angkor Wat each morning and spend the days moving about the temple complexes. I am reminded of Keo Narom: her sense of detachment is reflected in the neutral gaze in the sculptures of ancient Khmer rulers. Her hand gestures can be seen in the friezes of the Asparas—court dancers and female spirits of the clouds and water. They are carved in relief beside scenes of battle. The stone has been worn smooth and the surface glows like lacquer.

I return to Ta Prohm each afternoon. As evening falls, the temple sinks into semi-darkness. It is an in-between zone, a kind of No Man's Land. With a difference. There are no guns here and no barren stretches of hardened earth, no barbed wire or sentry posts. The space is sheltered and protected. I find secluded spots within the temple walls and on the fringe of the forest, where I can sit, close my eyes, and vanish.

Back in Phnom Penh, R drives me to Narom's house. She is waiting at the gate. She wears a blue sarong, a floral-patterned blouse and low-heeled shoes. We drive to a neighbourhood cafe. The streets are unusually quiet. It is the second day of a four-day mourning period leading up to Sihanouk's cremation. Many businesses and restaurants are closed.

The previous day, Sihanouk's embalmed body had been paraded through Phnom Penh in a gold casket on a circular route back to the palace and then beyond to the cremation stupa. The city had woken pre-dawn to the beat of drums, monks chanting, gamelan orchestras chiming, heralding a day of ceremony. Spectators crowded the length of the circuit, many dressed in white shirts, white blouses and white dresses: the colour of mourning.

The parade was a show of state might: the procession of floats and the gilded coffin chaperoned by the guards of the new order. Helmeted police patrolled, scanning the crowd, batons at the ready. Laughter erupted at the sight of a lone monkey brazenly strutting along the middle of the roadway, pausing to pose, expecting food in exchange for its performance.

The calm the next day is a sharp contrast. The trio is reunited: the teller, the listener and the interpreter. We are at ease, a reflection of the peace that has settled on the city on this public holiday, and of our growing camaraderie and sense of kinship. We are united in a common purpose. Narom is seated directly opposite me. There is a lightness in her being and a gentle rhythm in her telling.

She takes up her story where she had left off as we edged our way past the palace ten days earlier. Perhaps this is another reason for her lightness. She does not need to revisit the horrors. She resumes her account in Phnom Penh on 28 June 1975, her day of liberation.

She had returned to a metropolis where, in her absence, places of learning had been converted into prisons. Tuol Sleng, a primary school, had become a house of torment and interrogation. Now it is a museum of genocide. The dimly lit rooms contain the bricked-in cells and steel bedframes where the victims lay in between torture sessions, when they were driven to confess to the fabricated crimes their interrogators had assigned them.

The black-and-white mug shots of men, women and children are displayed on the walls of the converted classrooms where they were imprisoned. Their eyes are frozen in bewilderment. They stare at the blind eyes of a world that was going about its business as the killing continued. There was no one to save them.

On Narom's return, much of the city was intact, the outer layers still standing, but it was an empty shell. People picked over the rubble in search of photos and heirlooms, shards of what once was, something to grasp hold of. In the evenings, a hush fell over the streets and boulevards. The city was reawakening to life, but it would take a long time before it was restored to wholeness.

Before the Khmer Rouge ascendancy, Narom had studied and taught music at the School of Fine Arts. She played violin and *pipa* and taught notation and melody, but after the deaths of her children, she lost interest. She succumbed to days of torpor and hopelessness.

Many colleagues had died; some had gone insane. But it was an encounter with a former colleague, a professor of French, that helped jolt Narom back to the living. At first she did not recognise him. He walked about crazed and destitute. All he had been and once possessed—a sharp mind, a lust for life and delight in conversation—had vanished. In their place, there was an expression of incomprehension.

It was not this that shocked her; there were many like him. It was the recognition. In his haunted eyes, she saw her eyes. In his despair, she saw her despair. His presence was a reminder, and an accusation. She had a little sister—*ma petite soeur*—orphaned in a country of the orphaned. Hers was the new story, and the new year zero. Her sister needed guidance, and a way forward.

The word *healing* is too trite. Narom had survived, but it was a matter of luck. She entertains no simple notion of resilience. Hunger, disease, beatings, slave labour, exhaustion—and murderers—had not killed her, but they had killed many others, upwards of two million, one quarter of the population.

No one will ever know the exact figure. The landscape is dotted with mass graves. Eighty per cent of Cambodia's teachers and up to ninety per cent of its doctors, lawyers, engineers, civil servants, academics, artists and musicians lost their lives—an entire generation of professionals, along with its immense store of knowledge. The Khmer Rouge destroyed critical thinking, and in its place attempted to install blind allegiance. For Narom, it was not a healing, but a calculation, and when the costs were counted and weighed, it added up to an obligation.

Narom was invited to teach in the Ministry of Education. She trained as an ethnomusicologist and travelled the country in search of melodies. She spent time with indigenous groups and learnt about their instruments. As she describes them, her hands trace the shapes of the little-known instruments she came across in the provinces.

She sat in forest homes and listened. She spent time in the mountain regions and collected tales of genies and demons, sprites and forest spirits. She travelled to the eastern borderlands and compared the instruments of Vietnam and Cambodia. She returned to the western borderlands, the territory of her enslavement, and researched areas once occupied by the Thais, and again made comparisons.

She saw a deeper truth in the language of folklore and music, the commonalities that gave lie to the propaganda of ideologues and scoundrels. She understood the terror that lies in wait when leaders talk of purity and crude notions of blood and nation. Blueprints of Utopia: preludes to massacre, new killing fields.

In 2005, Narom published a book on the music of Cambodia. The title is embossed in gold lettering on a plain crimson cover. It has become a key reference for music scholars. She is extending her research to Laos, and working on a second volume. She has earned a doctorate exploring the complex relationship between the arts and sciences.

There was something else that saved her, she says. A return to Buddhist teachings and a growing sense of obligation to journey through life with purpose. It was either this or wither from despair. This, she says, is one of the reasons she had approached me during the afternoon tea break, two weeks earlier, with her story; and why she had given me permission to write it. Maybe what she had endured would be of value for others. Maybe it could act as a warning. She wanted future generations to be spared the horror. She wanted to alert them to the dangers.

In 2000, Narom took a new tack. There were children who lacked direction. They were the offspring of a lost generation. Outwardly their parents seemed well enough, but inside some were simmering. The anger could break out at any time, in bouts of violence and drinking, leading to family crises. Narom wrote fables for children, in the hope that people would not repeat the brutal ways of the Khmer Rouge and inherit their disregard for life and contempt for education and their hatred of those who loved the arts, sciences and humanities.

Keo Narom knows it is not over; the lust for power and wealth that drives people to commit murder is never over. She has sat with the children of post-Killing Fields generations, and understands their need for guidance. And she has found the language in which to express it: music and the written word, and the civilising power of knowledge.

She espouses simple homilies: Children, be grateful for the food you receive, lest you know real hunger. Children, be self-sufficient, know the value of work. Children, be aware of the hardship of those who live in the rural areas. Her resolve is evident as we sit, face to face, in this sunlit cafe, on a rare day of public quietude.

Light streams through the large windows. Light slips over our table. Light plays on the rims of Narom's glasses. Light creates space. It illumines the rings on her fingers, the flower motifs on her blouse, and the gold studs in her ears. It traces the ceaseless play of her hands, the looseness of her wrists and the suppleness of her fingers. It highlights the ridges between her eyes, and her pursed lips when she speaks of darker moments; and it accentuates a composure honed by years of endurance.

Her presence returns me to Ta Prohm, and the eerie calm that inhabits the ruins of fallen empires. And it takes me to No Man's Land, that barren stretch of dirt between fortified borders, and that uneasy walk forty-three years ago on the eve of a reign of terror. In No Man's Land, all hangs by a thread, all is reduced to the sound of a heartbeat. Guns point from both directions, holding each other at bay in an uneasy ceasefire. There is nowhere to hide. In No Man's Land all is transparent, stripped back to pure being.

In Keo Narom there is no self-pity and no false sentiment. Only when she talks of her children do her eyes well with tears. But they are quickly kept at bay with a gesture of the hand and an extension of her fingers, as if it would be a disservice to her children to falter. *En avance*, she says as we make our way back to R's car from the cafe. Always forward.

I think of Narom as I move about the city, on foot and on the backs of motorcycles, riding pillion passenger at peak hour, swerving in and out of traffic, absorbing the pulse of an expanding metropolis. There is no place for hesitation; a slight gap in the dense traffic, and the motorcyclists must go for it, or remain stranded.

Tables and chairs are lined up outside carpenters' workshops. Market stalls are piled high with sandstone and wood carvings of elephants and Angkor Wat replicas. Gangnam-style dancers are pictured on massive billboards. Women are at work in a cluster of florists' stalls. Their feet rock their babies' cribs, leaving their arms free to place flowers in intricate arrangements.

The struggle to exist is on open display. There is no concealment; the affluent possess that privilege. Beyond the mansions of the inner city and the five-star hotels and palaces down by the river, all is frenetic movement. Enclaves of destitution sprawl beside pockets of abundance, vast disparities in wealth and impoverishment heightened.

Yet there is energy and spirit, and songs of love and longing echoing like a muezzin's call over loudspeakers, couples walking hand in hand, couples speeding by on motorcycles, and children at play in massive schoolyards. My thoughts return to Narom, and the drive home, late afternoon, from the cafe. She stepped from the car outside her house, unlocked the gate, and headed for the front door.

It was then that I saw clearly what I had not noticed when we picked her up hours earlier. Narom's house, which she still lives in with her sister, is clad in steel and surrounded by barbed wire. Its windows are barred. It speaks of her abiding terror. How can it be otherwise?

I think of Keo Narom when I return to Cambodia in the following two years to conduct writing workshops in other cities. I think of her as I accompany four colleagues to the outskirts of Battambang for a meeting with a man who claims to be Voy Ho, a pre-Khmer Rouge-era songwriter.

Some say Voy Ho is no longer alive, and that he died during the Khmer Rouge era. Some say he has retreated to a life of contemplation. Others say he still writes songs under an alias. Word has come through. He has come to the city from his home in a Thai border village.

We turn off the main road and follow a clay path. Night is falling. Dogs bark in the gathering darkness. Children play hopscotch under street lamps. An elderly couple shuffles by. We pull up at a two-storey house. Voy Ho and his youngest daughter are at the door to greet us. He lifts his clasped hands in greeting.

The effects of a recent stroke are visible; he trails his right leg as he leads us into the house and up a stone stairway. We step into a large room, part storeroom, part bedroom, cluttered with cooking utensils, tins of oil, packaged food, boxes of cutlery, cooking pots and crockery.

The light is dim. The walls are bare except for a leather satchel hanging from a nail. A statuette of Buddha sits on a wooden shelf, suspended from the ceiling by wires threaded through the ventilation slats. A door opens out onto a tiny balcony overlooking the neighbourhood.

We sit in a circle on the tiled floor. Voy Ho folds his legs and settles himself in a lotus posture. He places a black leather case in front of him, unlatches the hinges and takes out a photo album, two exercise books, a grey-cloth diary and a tattered songbook.

A man of eighty, he wears a white shirt, khaki flannel-trousers and silver-rimmed glasses. His greying hair is close-cropped. A wisp of a beard sprouts beneath his chin. His face is disfigured by a purple scar. It extends from his forehead to his neck and upper chest, and continues beneath his shirt, where it can be glimpsed through the buttonholes.

Voy Ho speaks with a vigour that belies his age. He punctuates his speech with slaps on the floor and sudden bursts of hand gestures, then resumes his Buddha-like stillness. Shadows dart on the floor with each outburst. My companions are keenly focused on what he says. They want to make sure of his identity. The conversation is in Khmer, with some fragments translated for my benefit.

I am Voy Ho, he says. A writer of songs, renowned during the Golden Era, before the bombings and before the armies of Pol Pot marched into Phnom Penh. I had fame. I had wealth. My songs were played throughout the city and in Cambodian movies. They were performed on stage and on state television, and were loved by the people. Voy Ho recites some of his lyrics. This is the pattern of his talk: a cascade of anecdotes, remembrances and snatches of song, then a return to stillness.

The people thought I was dead, he says. They said the Khmer Rouge had murdered me, as they had murdered many songwriters and artists. I survived, but they killed me in other ways. Some people doubt my existence. They say I am not the real Voy Ho, and that I have assumed his identity. Rumour is stronger than truth. Speculation is preferred to reality.

He still writes, he says, pointing to his notebooks. Each song is dated, the first entry: 4 April 2010. No one in his home country performs his new songs. He now writes for Khmer singers who live and perform them across the Thai border. He is better known elsewhere. He directs us to insert a disc in the CD player that sits on a table beside us. These are my songs, he says, recorded in Thailand.

His four questioners seem to move between belief and suspicion. They flip through the pages of the diary and scrutinise his notebooks. They are on his side; they want to restore him to the pantheon of Cambodian songwriters. But they want to be sure. The tone of their questions edges towards interrogation.

Voy Ho is taken aback. His bursts of frustration are offset by deep-throated chuckles. In the dim light, his scar is softened. The album of photos is passed between his questioners. There are montages of singers, mics held to their lips, performing alongside a garlanded pianist, mini-skirted dancers, young men with bell-bottomed pants, and a singer with a beehive hairdo: markers of the late 60s and the early 70s.

Voy Ho produces evidence of the Khmer Rouge era: paper currency with images of a villager bearing an urn on his head, and a farmer in yellow shorts guiding a wooden plough drawn by a pair of bullocks. He takes two passport-sized photos from his wallet, one of him in his twenties, the other in his thirties. He points out a pre-Khmer Rouge photo of him in the album, as a young man in a suit jacket, his hair combed back from the forehead in an Elvis pompadour. His face is over exposed and the image is out of focus. This is me, he insists, stabbing his fingers at the photo. He is unflagging in his defence, defiant.

For three hours, the questioners persist. Voy Ho holds fast. He does not flinch. When we finally descend the stairs, I see him clearly in the downstairs light. The welt that extends down his left side is in stark contrast to the smoothness of his complexion on the right. Voy Ho's face is like the two sides of Janus: one facing a dark past, the other, an uncertain future. It reflects the brittle state of his nation. He accompanies us outside and embraces each of us at the doorway. We make our way back on the dirt path to the roadway.

Later, my companions debrief over an evening meal at a pavement restaurant. They remain uncertain, but the balance has shifted in Voy Ho's favour. There is talk of organising events in which he will be recognised and honoured. As we talk, one of our group points to the old cinema across the road where, in 1974, Khmer Rouge soldiers tossed a grenade into a crowded movie show.

He was a young boy on the day it happened. He saw the fleeing crowds, their panic, the carnage and mayhem. The trauma lingers. In Battambang the reminders are potent. This was a Khmer Rouge stronghold and a way-stop on Keo Narom's journey. The past is ever-present.

The following afternoon, one of the workshop convenors drives us six kilometres north to the outskirts of the city. The streets are quieter here. It is late afternoon. Children are on their way home from school, satchels slung over their shoulders. A farmer drives a cart loaded with watermelons; a cat scampers by and disappears into a vegetable garden.

P draws up to his home, a wooden house encircled by fruit trees. We make our way to the back garden beneath a canopy of palm leaves and banana fronds, to a back gate that opens directly onto a fairground with a mini Ferris wheel, rundown carousels and a miniature train—all dormant.

Beyond the fairground is a stream. A stone bridge leads to a clearing and a stupa, crowned by a spire that reaches to the heavens. Beneath the winged roof, on wooden shelves and encased in glass, are skulls and other bones. Engraved on one of the walls are the words: *The Well of Shadows.*

'In May 1976,' reads the inscription, 'the Khmer Rouge

seized the Buddhist Temple complex Wat Samrong Kong, turning it into a prison and an interrogation centre and the surrounding area into a killing field, where 10,008 people were put to death. The full extent of Cambodia's tragedy will never be known. The remains of some of the victims of this genocide may never be recovered, nor their murderers identified.'

The plinth of the stupa is adorned with bas-relief sculptures depicting the atrocities in confronting detail—the mass evacuations; the confiscation of possessions; slave labourers at work in rice paddies; children being herded away from their parents; enforced mass weddings; throats being slit with palm-leaf sinews; and figures being bludgeoned to death with axes and cudgels.

P's family were forced from their home in Battambang at about the same time as Keo Narom and her family left their home in Phnom Penh. When his family finally returned, they learnt that the area beside the house they had grown up in had been a site of mass killings. It has taken a long time to learn to live with it, says P, and to walk by the Well of Shadows without being outraged by reminders of the years of terror.

He pauses at the stupa, lights incense and makes an offering. There is a disorienting air of normality. Couples stroll by. Children ride bicycles in the clearing. Families are making their way to a festival in the temple precinct beyond the stupa. They cross a walkway overlooking a pond covered with lotuses.

The temple grounds are crowded. People mill around stalls selling offerings and trinkets. We climb the stone steps to the colonnaded foyer of the central pagoda. Inside, pilgrims light incense at the base of a massive statue of a Buddha seated on a carved wooden pedestal. We step onto the balcony. P and his companions purchase caged birds which they release over the parapet. The same birds will be recaptured, returned to crowded cages and released again in an endless ritual of liberation and imprisonment.

As evening falls, the fairground springs to life. The food stalls are lit up and the Ferris wheel and carousels are in motion. We return via the back gate to the veranda of P's house, where his family is gathered. The day's work is over. We eat and chat. Our voices rise into a languid night. All appears normal.

But sometimes, when I lie in my bed at night, says P, I hear the souls of the dead children. They are laughing, and playing. I cannot breathe. I cannot bear it.

P drives us back to central Battambang. 'It's not over,' says Y, later that night over dinner. 'It did not end with the Killing Fields. You cannot finish the story with Pol Pot. You cannot cut one time off from another. The conflict continues in new guises. It has never ended.'

Y is in his twenties, an aspiring writer. He had attended the first workshop in Phnom Penh, and has helped organise the workshop in Battambang. He wears tight-fitting jeans and a black T-shirt with designer label motifs. He is strongly built, and exudes strength and a ferocious energy. He speaks with intensity. 'The dust has not settled,' he says.

It was in his village, deep in the forests, that he first heard of the black-clad cadres, as his grandfather, grandmother, uncles and aunts, and neighbours talked late at night. Y lay close to sleep and heard fragments. He could not make out which brother had turned on brother, who had been slave and who had held the whip, who had been victim or perpetrator.

Outside the wind blew through the forests. It was the familiar music of the night and the melody of his childhood. The trees bore witness. They had survived in far greater numbers than the people. When the killing times were over, the villagers returned to their most precious possession, the forest. It was the source of their meagre living and the sacred grounds of their ancestors—a home to spirits and deities, and to cheeky gibbons and a choir of bullfrogs.

The bulldozers stole in during the night. The villagers woke to chainsaws and trees falling. They registered each thud as the death of a fallen comrade. They were being stripped of their livelihoods and their trusted companions. Where once were trees, there are now ghosts, says Y.

At night, the ghosts inhabit the emptied spaces. They can be heard moving about, as can the disoriented animals. They are sniffing the air, seeking new shelter and retreating ever deeper into remaining enclaves of forest. The sound of their amiable chatter is fading. The melody of the forest is being silenced.

Where the forest once stood, says Y, the land stretches desolate to the horizon. Day and night, trucks piled high with logs drove to the borderlands, protected by the police and military, the profits returned to the few who hold the levers of power. Why do my people remain so destitute? Y asks. He seethes at the injustice. His people had been orphaned twice over, robbed of their families and, now, of their forests.

The young men and women of the village were enraged, but powerless. At the best of times their families barely made a living. With the death of the forest, there was little work for them in their barren homelands. They yearned to get out and explore the world beyond. They made their way over the mountain roads to the cities. The journey began on foot, and continued by motorbike. As the roads widened, they travelled by bus, passing remnants of forest in dust-ridden wastelands.

Y tells me of his anger and his efforts to tame it, and the warring inner voices pitted against each other. 'Use your mind, not your body. Present your case. Tell the story.' 'This is easy to say,' the opposing voice replies. 'Thousands of hectares have been stolen, livelihoods trashed, dreams trampled, and our stories have not saved us.'

For now, the stories have won out. He stands in front of the workshop participants and reads extracts of his work. He is an expressive storyteller and a natural performer, his intensity allayed by detours into humour. He stands tall and straight. His muscular shoulders and chest are open. He is streetwise, and burns with a yearning for experience. He is sorting it out, weighing it up, as are many of his generation. Looking forward.

And Keo Narom listens. She talks with Y in the breaks, and connects with the younger writers. She is at ease in their company, and at one with their passion. She too stands and reads her stories. She is *Nak Kruu* Keo Narom, a revered teacher in a country in desperate need of elders. Her quiet, insistent voice commands attention. Use the power of your mind, she says. Travel the country, she urges, and come to know your people.

I am reminded of Narom's passion as I travel on provincial roads and highways—in the stone masons' works-in-progress lined up on the roadsides, Buddhas in meditation postures alongside the busts of famed rulers of Khmer kingdoms; in stalls piled high with mangos, watermelons and pineapples, the tropical trinity; in the fishing villages jutting out from the banks of the Mekong; and in the bobbing boats of the river nomads.

In the ring of coconut trees, bent inwards, like a circle of whispering conspirators; in the young men in footpath garages mending motorcycles with the loving attention of mothers tending new-born babies. In the hammocks slung in the cool spaces beneath village homes; and in the young woman seated on the stoop of a hut, mirror in hand, combing her waist-length hair, just metres from a dirt pathway.

And I think of her as I am driven to the garment district, on the outskirts of Phnom Penh in the late afternoon, mid-January 2014. Workers in the thousands are making their way home over unpaved roads. Dust clings to their clothes and around the workers' hostels and apartment buildings. My host pulls his car up to the gates of the Canadia Industrial Park. It was here, he says, two weeks ago, that thousands of striking textile workers assembled, after marching in protest at their one-hundred-dollar-a-month wages and Dickensian work conditions.

The rage erupted. Workers battled riot police and security forces. Stones and Molotov cocktails were pitted against steel batons, and a burst of gunshot from AK-47 rifles. The protesters turned and ran. They were pursued through the billowing smoke. They dodged burning barricades and ducked beneath bullets.

They fled past the dead and the wounded, fending off beatings, seeking refuge in the back streets and neighbouring houses.

Now, weeks later, the post-work trek continues, as it has for years. Each evening, weary men and women in the thousands, on foot and on bicycles, make their way home as if in a trance. Others crowd the trays of trucks returning them to the villages they had left at sunrise. Those seated on the edge dangle their legs over the highway. Their bodies jolt with each lurch of the truck, each pothole.

A city of dust is giving way to dusk, and still workers pour out of the factory gates, and my thoughts return to Keo Narom, her journey through a broken country, consumed by sorrow, and her epic trek back to her wounded city. I try to imagine her unfathomable grief, and the resurrection of her spirit; and her return, years later to the sites of her loss and terror—notebook and recorder in hand, and the people gathered about her gifting her their music.

I see her at the gate of her house, turning to wave, then disappearing into her steel-clad haven—my last sight of her; and I think of the gift she has given me, the doors she has opened for me, allowing me a glimpse of her beloved country. And of the gentle spirit that, despite it all, resides within her.

There is a coda to this tale that demands to be told, an uncanny parallel. I sensed the resemblance when we first met: in Keo Narom's fine complexion and dyed black hair, and in her innate beauty and unobtrusive manner. She reminded me of Hadassah, my mother, in her times of serenity.

Hadassah, like Narom, had lost her entire family—except for two sisters—to genocide. Unlike Narom, she did not experience the carnage directly. She left in time, but the damage was irrevocable. Hadassah's youthful ideals of brotherhood and sisterhood had been violated. Her descents into despair could occur at any time. She could never speak of what had happened to them, but wept over her impotence to save them.

For Hadassah, too, there was a time before, a childhood lived in the border town of Grodek, and a youth spent in the city of Bialystok, where she performed at community celebrations as a singer of Yiddish song: a public presence in a time of belonging and purpose.

Unlike Narom, in the new world, Hadassah's public voice was silenced. She could not allow herself the joy of celebration. Nor did she have the time or energy. She worked in the new city, helping her husband at his Victoria Market stall and at her sewing machine, late into the night, stitching clothes for the factories of Brunswick and Flinders Lane, Melbourne's garment district.

She was confined to singing at home as she cleaned and cooked, washed and sewed, and looked after the three sons who were born after the Annihilation. She channelled whatever will she had left into raising her children. In this she was heroic, fierce in her resolve. Defiant.

And she sang. For hours on end, her mezzo-soprano edged by anguish. Her repertoire was vast. Lullabies and laments. Love songs. Nonsense songs. Children's songs. Ballads of gypsies and miraculous goats. Hymns of protest and revolt.

Songs of praise for the borderlands of her native Poland. Songs of toil and labour:

> *And you plough and you hoe, tend your herd, and you sew. And you hammer and weave, tell me, what pittance do you receive? And you extract ore from the shaft, and harvest wheat thick with chaff. But tell me, where is your table set? Where is your festive dress? Where is your sharpened sword? Where is the joy that you deserve?*

Hadassah was never again able to practise her vocation. She retreated from the world. She was unable to overcome her sense of life as a betrayal and find solace for her wounded spirit. Unable to overcome her unjustified guilt for not saving her loved ones. She could not forgive herself for surviving, and would not allow her talents to flourish. Strange to say, in meeting Keo Narom, I saw what could have been…

Republic of the Stateless

Sonia Lizaron is waiting. She is neatly dressed in a pale-blue skirt and matching jacket. Her face is powdered and her cheeks are rouged. She is ninety-five years old, in aged care. After the death two years ago of her partner Pinche Wiener, she was transferred to the dementia ward, though she is far from demented. She is the Sonia I have known for more than three decades: unassuming, dignified and, for the most part, tranquil.

On the wall hangs the sleeve of Sonia's album of Yiddish songs, '*In Freyd un Umet*', 'In Joy and Sorrow'. Her face adorns the cover. She is radiant. She wears bright red lipstick, eye-shadow and mascara, and an off-the-shoulder black dress with gold trimming.

Beside the cover hang two portraits of Sonia, one painted in New York, the other in Paris, and, stuck to the wall with Blu Tack are Sonia's drawings: a tree, a bird, and the traced outline of her hand and wrist encircled by an orange bangle. On a coffee table stands a vase of roses, and on the dresser, two pre-war photos of Sonia's mother, Lisa, one with her two young children: her son, Genek, and daughter, Sonia.

The dementia ward is in the basement. Sonia sits in an armchair, on the bedside table, within reach, a box of tissues and a transistor radio. A Shostakovich string quartet is playing. Sonia's eyes are closed and she sways to the music. A window opens out into a courtyard, enclosed on four sides by several storeys. There are plants, and there is light; but the courtyard is hemmed in, claustrophobic.

Sonia is not affected. She knows how to withstand confined spaces. She possesses infinite patience. She knows how to endure a state of prolonged transience. She had long ago developed the ability to dismiss thoughts that are disturbing. There are questions she deflects and places she no longer ventures. She has mastered the art of the moment, and in this moment there is only music.

When I enter, she opens her eyes and searches my face for recognition. Then she lights up: '*Arelle der narelle*,' she says. 'Little Aron the little fool'—a cheeky term of endearment. She stretches the vowels for emphasis. Then chuckles. We converse in Yiddish. In recent years, she has moved back in time through her languages from English to French, Russian and Polish and, finally, Yiddish, the mother tongue.

'How are you?' I ask. 'Hanging in there,' she replies. It is her ritual response. She sings: '*Vos geven, is geven, un nishto*'. What was, once was, and is no more. But what 'once was' remains extraordinary. Sonia lived an epic life, but rarely spoke about it, save the few recurring stories she told me over the years, and her occasional comments on an album of photos depicting a theatre troupe, post-war, in the displaced persons camp, Bergen-Belsen.

Sonia hung in there, in the dementia ward, for another five months. She hung in there even after she slipped into her final coma. She died two weeks later. As we sat by her body late into the night, one of her closest friends made a profound observation.

Sonia endured for so long because she had been in this situation before. Her body had learnt to cope with deprivation. The memory of it was a part of her being.

It is said there are stories that are meant to be told and that not to tell them would be to betray them. This is one such story.

May 2018. The house is gone. In its place, behind a cyclone fence, a vacant lot strewn with mounds of clay and dirt, thistles and wild grasses. A row of cypress line the back fence, and a block of flats and houses mark the side boundaries. The lot is up for auction. 'A rare townhouse opportunity', reads the real-estate board.

Here, at 18 Joyce Street Elwood, stood the house built by the Wiener brothers, Bono and Pinche, of solid brick, rock-hard foundations. It was in this house, in the mid 1980s, that I first met Sonia. It takes time for the mind to adjust and re-imagine the layout as it once was: the untidy front garden, the car parked askew in the driveway, the small entrance porch and doorbell; and the expectant pause before Sonia and Pinche answered.

Whenever I visited with my partner they were pleased to see us, more so after 1993, when our son was born. Their faces would be beaming. 'The no-good bastard is here,' says Pinche, pointing at me. My infant son is pleased to hear him say it.

To the right of the hallway stands the master bedroom, and to the left, through the double doors, an open-plan living room. Leather swivel chairs and sofas surround a glass-topped coffee table stacked with newspapers, books and journals. This was often a place of heated conversation and political argument. The

Wiener brothers lived life with passion.

On the wall, a large TV screen—the world news; and on a sideboard, a record player, and beside it a stack of vinyl records. The floor-to-ceiling shelves are crowded with ornaments and sculptures collected by Bono on his extensive travels, and the walls are lined with paintings of shtetl scenes, Chagall prints and Yosl Bergner originals. The living room opens into an elevated dining space.

The kitchen smells of herring, black bread and garlic. On the wall above the phone, hangs a calendar, dates marked with appointments and engagements. A rear door leads to an office; the desk is scattered with bills and books in a Babel of languages. The back window overlooks a backyard swimming pool in which the Wiener brothers and Sonia swim every morning.

It was from this house that Sonia and Pinche made their final move to the aged-care home, trading the independence they so treasured for security as they approached their nineties. Bowing, proudly, to the inevitable.

There is something else that comes to mind at the vacant lot: Sonia and Pinche as I saw them one windy day, setting out on their afternoon walk to the foreshore. I retrace their steps from the lot, right into St Kilda Street, and one block south to Beach Road, pausing at the traffic lights by the corner nursery.

They cross the road and make their way along the gravel path through the foreshore parklands. Pinche strides forward, straining with each determined step. Sonia, unconcerned, maintains her own pace. The argument on this has long been settled.

Neither of them bends, but there is a compromise. Pinche pulls ahead for a while, then returns. Again, they walk together. This is the pattern: an alternating between fierce independence and reliance.

Pinche and Sonia walk past the familiar markers: the croquet club, the park with its cropped lawns and playing fields. Mid-afternoon it is quiet, bar the whoosh of traffic on the highway. Perhaps too quiet. At the end of Head Street stands a solitary palm. They step out to the sea air, and in that instant, Sonia's longing for her native Lodz, or for Paris and New York, her adopted cities, is swept away by the glorious present.

This is the reason she chose to live her final years here, at the ends of the earth. This daily miracle: the sweep of the bay, the sun on the silver water, freighters heading to and from the docks, and the nearby marina filled with boats, masts naked in their winter hibernation. And all this a ten-minute walk from the house in Joyce Street.

The couple turn onto the seaside walkway and join the stream of joggers, strollers, other elderly couples and power walkers. Cyclists are racing by. Why the hurry? Why not enjoy the rhythmic wash of waves, and the congregations of dog-walkers, their pets sniffing each other while the owners compare notes on their red setters, Samoyeds and greyhounds?

Sonia and Pinche begin the return under reddening skies, past the octagonal kiosk, the sailing club, the anglers club, the life-saving club, each with their insignia. The walk is taxing. Their shadows lengthen before them. Darkness is falling as they turn back into Head Street. Again, Pinche leads the way. The house lights are switching on. Through the windows can be seen flickering TV screens, private enclaves of intimacy. Beach Road vibrates with peak-hour traffic. One block further on the couple turn left, and into the house on Joyce Street: a haven.

Long before Pinche there was someone else. On one of my last visits to Sonia, I showed her a photo of Sami Feder. 'Yes. I knew him,' she says. 'Sami. He was my husband.' She shrugs her shoulders, closes her eyes, and runs her fists over them. 'Ah, you look so beautiful today,' she says, when she reopens her eyes and gazes at her visitors. In that moment, we are all that matters.

In the years that I knew her, I never saw Sonia cry. She maintained a vigil against painful memories. She was resolute. The closest she allowed herself to come to tears was in that gesture: she would close her fists and brush the back of the knuckles over her eyelids. Then she would reopen them and return, fully alert, to the present.

We sit in her room. The conversation drifts in and out between comfortable silences. '*Ikh heib zikh oif vider un shpan avek veiter,*' I say. 'I lift myself up and again stride onward.' Sonia takes it up and recites the entire poem, as she has many times. This will be the last time, just weeks before she slipped into her final coma. She performs the lines with her eyes closed. Her recitation skills remain intact. They are second nature.

Di velt nemt mikh arum mit stekhike hent,
Un trogt mikh tsum feyer, un trogt mikh tsum shayter;
Ikh bren un ikh bren un ikh ver nit farbrent—

Ikh heib zikh oif vider un shpan avek veiter.

The world embraces me with barbed hands,
And carries me to the fire, and to the pyre;
I burn and I burn, but I am not consumed—
I lift myself up, and again, stride onwards.

Sonia Lizaron was born Sonia Boszkowska in Lodz, on 1 May 1919. Lodz was an industrial city, the skyline dominated by tall brick chimneys. Textile workers laboured in cavernous rooms with grime-stained windows. Mechanised looms beat their round-the-clock rhythm. Trolleys filled with clothing clattered over wooden bridges and porters walked the streets, bent under the heavy packs tied to their shoulders. Travelling salesmen sat late into the night, sealing deals, talking business.

Sonia's father, Aron Boszkowski, was an accountant in a textile factory. He, and Sonia's mother Lisa, were members of the Jewish Labour Bund. In inter-war Poland, the Bund was a mass workers' movement with representation in both local and national governments. Sonia imbibed the Bund ideals of *Yiddishkayt*, a secular humanism driven by a yearning for social justice and a love of the Yiddish language as the earthy expression of the people.

In her youth, she trained as an actor and singer with Moyshe Broderson, the founder of the *Kleynkunst* theatre, Ararat, named after the mountain where Noah's Ark was said to be grounded, and doubling as the acronym for the Artistic Revolutionary Revue Theatre.

Kleynkunst, literally 'small art', is the art of Yiddish cabaret, and Broderson was one of its leading exponents. A man about town, with a mane of black hair and Pushkin-style sideburns, Broderson was often seen dressed in a black shirt, affecting the demeanour of a Russian worker. He wore amber and coral necklaces, and rings on each finger. He held court in literary cafes and walked the streets accompanied by a retinue of hangers-on and colleagues. A master of wordplay, he compered cabaret shows in rhyming couplets sprinkled with puns, parodies and political satire.

Broderson founded a drama studio, and revelled in his role as teacher and mentor. He was impressed by Sonia's talent and encouraged her to pursue a vocation as a singer and actor. His students could never have imagined that the theatre, and the culture that nurtured it, would soon be threatened with annihilation.

Sonia made her acting debut in Lodz as the storm clouds of war were gathering. Her mother had died of cancer before the outbreak of war. When the Germans occupied Lodz, Sonia was deported with her father and brother to Bedzin, a city in Upper Silesia, territory annexed by the Germans. Bedzin was a textile centre. Its confiscated factories were essential to the war effort, producing uniforms for the German army. The expertise of Bedzin's Jewish textile workers granted them a reprieve when a section of the city was converted into a ghetto. It was in Bedzin that Sonia met Sami Feder.

Sami was born on 5 December 1906, in the Polish city of Zawiercie, in Silesia. His father, Eliezer, a textile worker, died in a factory accident when Sami was three. His mother, Golda-Rivke, a seamstress, was left with five young children. Sami was adopted by his maternal grandfather, Ephraim-Fishl Imerglik, a watchmaker. In 1918, Ephraim-Fishl took Sami to live with him in Frankfurt am Maine in Germany, where Sami attended a Yiddish folk school, a German high school and a Yeshiva for religious studies.

Sami fell in love with the stage as a teenager. He joined the Sholem Aleichem Club and worked with its drama circle to produce Yiddish classics. He studied acting and directing at night school, and attended lectures on Yiddish language and literature. When the renowned Habimah Theatre toured Frankfurt, he watched every performance. He stood behind the curtain and studied each movement and gesture. His dedication was noted by the theatre's artistic director, Zvi Friedland.

Friedland invited him to study in his Berlin Yiddish Theatre Studio. Sami was drawn into the maelstrom of Weimar Berlin. His mentors included Austrian theatre director Max Reinhardt, German theatre producer Erwin Piscator and Soviet director Alexander Granowski.

Feder graduated as an actor and performed in several Berlin theatre companies. He worked as a journalist, translator and dramaturge, wrote articles for progressive literary journals and co-published the Yiddish weekly *Die Neue Zeit*. He was active in Berlin's Actors and Artists Union and founded a Yiddish labourers' troupe, bringing to it the innovations of the European Art Theatre movement. He made a living setting Yiddish type in a printing workshop.

When the Nazis came to power in 1933, Feder was

blacklisted as a stateless Jew of the political left. His room was ransacked by the SS, and he went into hiding. He fled to Poland, to Warsaw, where he warned Yiddish writers and journalists of Hitler's murderous intent.

Disillusioned by their complacent response, Feder turned to the theatre. He enlisted dramaturg Shmuel Volman, who was well versed in Warsaw Yiddish dialect, to co-write *Hitleriada*, a satire on the Führer, which was also titled *In This World, Nothing Changes*. Feder worked in the Berlin tradition that nurtured him, viewing theatre as a craft at the service of a higher end. He defined his pre-war Polish-based theatre work as 'careful art', interweaving anti-Hitler texts into cabaret acts to disguise their subversive intent.

Feder premiered the satire in Warsaw with the Orpheus Drama group, and worked with local drama groups to stage it in provincial towns. After a disturbance at a performance of *Hitleriada* in the town of Otwock, he was advised by the Polish police to leave Warsaw or risk imprisonment.

Sami returned to his mother's town, in the Zaglembie region, in southern Poland. After lying low for a while, he was invited to direct the Bedzin Muze Theatre and the *Lire* drama circle in the nearby city of Sosnowiec. Undeterred, he restaged *Hitleriada*. He continued to work with Muze after the Nazis occupied and annexed Benzin, and it was during this time that Sami met Sonia, who was performing in the Muze Theatre.

Sami Feder's impact on Sonia was profound. His view of theatre as a means of easing the suffering of his people in dark times was in accord with her Bund upbringing and her work in the subversive art of Yiddish cabaret. Sami directed Sonia in several productions. But his time with Muze was cut short when, in May 1941, he was deported to Germany and interned in a slave labour camp.

Hence began a journey through twelve concentration camps, or, as Feder describes it in one of his memoirs, 'through twelve portals of hell'. Sami did not stop his cultural work. Even in the darkest of times he organised performances. In Bunzlau slave labour camp he produced evenings of theatre, adapting excerpts from Yiddish classics that reflected the predicament of his fellow prisoners.

Theatre was an act of resistance, performed openly if possible, or, when need be, in secret, in barracks transformed into performance spaces. The texts were recalled from memory. Feder disguised his intent by playing on Jewish stereotypes to appease his captors. His audiences of inmates understood the ruse. In later years, he would define his theatre as frontline art and, as the title of one of his memoirs has it, the art of the Closed Fist. Sami recounts:

> Our hope for a theatre was born in the late-night hours after a long day of slave labour and whippings. We had nothing, and that was our strength. Not even a pencil, a piece of paper. Only a feeling in our hearts. I would hear people humming a melody...these melodies would not let go of me. They possessed so much pain and suffering... they grew in my mind into a vision which I could not put into words.

> On a Sunday night, when the Gestapo dogs finally let us be, we would creep down from our bunks, shift the tables, and get to work. We would forget that we were in a concentration camp. We created backdrops and curtains from our mattresses. We made up our faces with the ash of burnt matches. And that is how it started...The audience gave us cigarette butts, the highest tribute we could have expected.

In May 1942, Sonia's father and brother were herded into a train bound for the extermination camp Auschwitz. Years later, Sonia told me an extraordinary tale. Although not selected for deportation, she hurried to the station to join them against the objections of Alfred Rossner, the German textile factory manager for whom she worked. She could not bear the thought of separation.

Rossner drove his one-horse buggy to the station and searched frantically for Sonia. The platform was patrolled by armed SS men, but Rossner's status as a factory manager engaged in the war effort allowed him to move about freely. He found Sonia inside a crowded wagon as the train was about to leave. He dragged her onto the platform, knocked her out, lifted her into the buggy, and drove her back to the factory.

Aron and Genek perished. Sonia was one of many ghetto inmates Rossner saved from deportation. He was revered for his concern for his workers. He shielded them from the SS, arranged escapes and warned them of impending deportation. He sent his German workers to the station to rescue them from the transports and provided escapees with refuge in his workshop. Rossner was arrested by the Gestapo towards the end of 1944 and executed by hanging. Over the years, Sonia spoke often of his goodness.

Sonia did not waste her reprieve. She continued performing in the Bedzin Ghetto in sketches of ghetto life, and recited texts detailing the suffering of the inmates, written by her friend Sofia Shpiglman, who was later murdered in Auschwitz. The performances were frowned on by the Judenrat, the Jewish council appointed by the Nazis to do their bidding. The Judenrat feared the negative impact the recitations might have on the inmates. The council members did not understand, as did Sonia, that performance was a means of lifting morale in desperate times: a form of resistance.

Out of the thirty thousand inmates of the Bedzin Ghetto, an estimated two thousand survived. The ghetto was liquidated in August 1943. Sonia was deported to the slave labour camp Annaberg and then to the Mauthausen concentration camp in Austria. In January 1945, she was marched to the transit camp Bergen-Belsen in northern Germany. Despite the horror, she sang for some of the prisoners. She was among the thousands liberated by British troops on 15 April 1945.

The soldiers were horrified at the scenes that met them. Thousands of unburied corpses lay piled in the huts, in the doorways and scattered over the camp grounds. Inmates, infested with fleas and lice, huddled in the squalid huts shrunken to skeletons, dressed in rags, covered in filth and vomit, unable to move, even at the sight of their liberators. Men and women crawled through the mud and rose to their knees to kiss the hands and feet of British soldiers.

The camp housed Jehovah's Witnesses, Roma and Sinti, homosexuals, prisoners of war from many nations and, for the most part, Jews transported from Poland, Greece, Holland and Hungary and from slave labour and death camps throughout Germany and its occupied territories.

The bulk of the inmates, upwards of sixty thousand, were in Camp 1, dubbed the Horror Camp by British soldiers. Among them Sonia. Fifteen thousand prisoners of war were liberated from Camp 2, in the military barracks of the Panzer training school for German officers. Among them Sami.

More than thirty-five thousand inmates died in the ten months before liberation. Upwards of thirteen thousand were to die in the first five weeks after liberation, from many illnesses: typhus, tuberculosis, malnutrition and dysentery, and from over-eating; their shrunken digestive systems were unable to cope after months of starvation. Sonia rarely spoke to me of this period.

Perhaps she was among the liberated women who raided the SS stores in search of clothes and make-up. They applied rouge, powder and lipstick to their gaunt faces to regain a sense of womanhood, and perfumes to negate the stench of confinement. The women were frantic. The make-up was as vital as food in returning their skeletal bodies to the living.

The British military ordered squads of SS men and women and German soldiers and civilians to load the bodies onto trucks and carts and transport them to pits for mass burial in the southwest corner of the camp. The sick and infested were scrubbed and deloused, issued new clothing, and provided with medical support. The inmates of Camp 1 were transported to the displaced persons camp, set up in the spacious grounds of the Panzer training school.

By 18 May, the evacuation was complete. British troops burnt the barracks of Camp 1 to the ground to prevent the further spread of disease. The last huts were destroyed in a ceremony on 21 May. A crowd of British soldiers and former inmates stood by and rejoiced as the camp was engulfed by flames. The physical destruction of the Horror Camp was finished; but the restoration of desire and hope had barely started.

In Bergen-Belsen, Sonia was reunited with Sami. They became foundation members of the camp's Jewish Central Committee, and its culture department. Sonia joined Sami in creating a camp-based theatre. In one of the few stories she told me, Sonia said that she rode a bicycle through the camp in search of people with theatre skills, and invited them to join the newly formed ensemble. She cycled from block to block through the camp, which housed thousands.

The theatre drew in performers, musicians, artists, writers, tailors and technicians. Its members appropriated drapes from the British officers' quarters to make costumes. They scavenged for props and make-up in nearby towns and villages, and they bartered cigarettes in exchange for reels of thread, timber and nails, materials and musical instruments. Sonia Boszkowska, Sami Feder, set-designer Berl Friedler and his wife, choreographer and dancer Dolly Kotz, were among the leading lights. Sami was the driving force.

The group first met on 14 July in classrooms the British

had converted into an English language school. The venture was initially called *Di Dramatishe Studye*, the Drama Studio, and served as a school to enhance the skills of former actors and to train those with little performance experience. Sami conducted workshops on mime and rhythm, and gave lectures on literature and theatre history.

The studio was renamed the *Kazet Theatre*, the Concentration Camp Theatre, in honour of the actors who had performed under Feder's direction in the camps and ghettos, many of whom had perished. Some of those who survived became key members of the ensemble. 'Our duty,' proclaimed the theatre banner, 'is to spread light and culture.'

Sonia assisted Sami in gathering stories. She went from bed to bed in the camp hospital and collected testimonies from survivors. She retrieved and sang Yiddish songs, which were notated and adapted for performance. The works, compiled by Sami Feder and his collaborators, were published in 1946, titled: *Zamlung fun Kazet un Ghetto Lieder*, An Anthology of Songs and Poems from the Concentration Camps and Ghettos.

On the cover of the booklet is a watercolour of a skeletal figure. He wears white prison pants. His upper body is naked and his head is shaven. He is on his knees, back arched, arms outstretched, his bound hands reaching for the burning heavens. He is breaking free of the flames and the barbed wire that entangles him.

The anthology is illustrated by Berl Friedler: an inmate in striped prison clothes lies curled on the ground, his face twisted in a grimace; leather-booted men wield whips and rifles; a weeping woman kneels under the weight of the heavy load of her labour; an emaciated man huddles in an overcoat. Three men hang from the gallows before an assembly of prisoners, heads bowed, their bodies melded into an amorphous mass of figures. Two prisoners lie in a dark cell, beneath a tiny barred window; wounded slave-labourers stagger past electrified fences beneath guard towers. There are drawings of beatings and humiliations and photographs of intertwined corpses on the day of liberation.

The works are written by both unknown authors and established poets. A sense of rage and abandonment pervades them. Mothers weep for their lost children; inmates grieve the murders of their loved ones and the annihilation of entire communities. Lone men and women are driven to madness by the loss of their families.

The crimes are explicit: the deportations, the rapes and the mass disposal of bodies in crematoria. There are verses that depict the hunger that reduces men and women to jealous rages over an extra potato peel in the soup of a fellow prisoner; and the treachery of turncoats who tried to save their skins by doing the bidding of their captors.

The suffering is too recent to be watered down. To do so would be a betrayal. 'Remember this,' Feder writes in the foreword. 'We sing these songs as a memory—and a warning.' The works were the backbone of the ensemble's initial performances.

The Kazet Theatre premiered on 6 September in a theatre tent, just metres from the site where thousands of inmates who had died from illness in the weeks after liberation were buried. The tent was erected in 1940 by the German military, the canvas stretched taut across aluminium girders. It housed a stage, a proscenium arch, backstage facilities and an underground heating system. Goebbels and Goering are said to have used the venue to lecture officers of the military academy.

An audience of three thousand crowded into a space that could accommodate one thousand. British officers and their secretaries stole in through the stage door; they would not move, despite Feder's entreaties. Russian officers who had travelled two hundred kilometres to see the show demanded entrance. After a heated argument, Feder agreed to let them watch from the wings.

The many survivors who could not gain entrance jostled by the canvas, pleading and weeping. They had been denied so much for so long, the thought of missing out was unbearable. Thinking a mass demonstration was under way, British soldiers called for tanks to restore order. The stage was packed with those who had stolen in by a rear entrance. They had to be cleared before the performance could begin. The actors shouted their lines in the early scenes to be heard over the rumble of tanks and jeeps and the cries of the crowd outside.

The response of the audience was immediate and visceral. Many wept throughout the production. Some screamed and shouted, others became hysterical. The performers and the audience were barely distinguishable. They formed a single entity in their expression of loss and grief, offering it up as if in sacrifice to the gods of theatre. The space was reminiscent of the amphitheatres of ancient Greece, returning drama to its origins, as a ritual of communal release: an exorcism.

The actors did not portray themselves as victims. They did

not shy away from re-enactments of their recent experiences. Given the horrors of the recent past it could not be otherwise. There was no longer a need for careful theatre, and no desire for subterfuge. The stage was a safe space. The impact was cathartic. At the end of the performance the audience fell into a prolonged silence.

There is a photo of twenty-two members of the troupe dressed in striped prison clothes. They are gathered in front of a stage set headed *Eine Laus. Dein Tod!* One Louse. Your Death! replicating the backdrop for Feder's performers in the Bunzlau slave labour camp. The shadows of those in the back row fall on a white backdrop. Sami and Sonia can be made out, seated side by side in the centre row, but no one occupies pride of place.

The performers lean on each other. They look directly at the viewer. Their expressions are earnest and confronting. Ghostly almost. The trauma is writ on their faces, as too is a collective strength and a sense of defiance. We are here, they seem to say. Take us or leave us. We are not afraid to be seen as we are. One day we may go our separate ways. We may voyage to distant lands and build new lives, but in this moment in time we are here, and we are as one. We bear witness to ourselves, and we bear witness to each other. And in our being and our presence, we bear witness to our audience of survivors. When they see us on stage, they see themselves.

The Kazet Theatre rotated two programs in cabaret format—monodramas, songs, poems and dances, and dramatic sketches.

One sketch, 'This Is How It Began', depicts the brutal round-ups, the intimidation and the initial incarceration in the ghettoes and death camps. Others depict the counterattack: acts of sabotage and espionage, uprisings and daring rescues.

In Sami Feder's one-act play 'Partisans', Sonia performs the role of a resistance fighter who makes her way to Warsaw disguised as a cabaret singer. She infiltrates the German high command, sings in a low-cut black gown for an SS officer, and gains access to a cache of arms, which she steals for her band of partisans. The weapons are used to liberate a convoy of ghetto inmates bound for the death camps; the freed prisoners are transformed from listless slaves into fighters.

The Kazet Theatre used the symbols of Nazi persecution—SS insignias, the swastika, and prison garb—in the design of its costumes, stage sets and posters. A solo dance, choreographed by Dolly Kotz, depicts the pain of mothers torn from their children. Dolly performs in a striped prison dress in front of a black flag with a swastika enclosed in a white circle.

She cuddles an infant in her arms. As the baby is snatched away, her body contorts with pain. Her eyes are shut tight, and her face is a study of grief and unbearable longing. The horror cannot be diluted. The baby is bound for the crematorium. The murder of children is the greatest atrocity, and the deepest ache. It defies comprehension.

Sonia Boszkowska was the Kazet Theatre's leading performer. Her signature act was Sami Feder's poem *Ikh bin a shotn,* I am a shadow. The poem is dedicated to Sonia. Sami writes beneath the title: *For Sonia, my comrade, a present.* Sonia recites the poem in a white gown, her face white with make-up. Her arms are spread wide, and her open palms are turned upwards.

She is backed by a painting of a shapeless shadow rising from the stage floor, assuming the form of a monster as it widens: *'I am a shadow on the world/ Like a shadow I lie on my bed.../ Existing in a dream/ Everything that was/ Everything I once knew is gone/ I cannot cry nor laugh.../ I do not even know what prayer I should make.../ What lamentations I should weep/ What Kaddish I should recite...*

The gigantic head and massive shoulders of the shadow tower over Sonia. The head is bent forward, and the arms and hands form a grasping gesture. The contrast between the black mass and the figure in white accentuates the menace.

But Sonia stands undaunted. She appears detached, despite the horrors she is recounting: *Oh, curse their bones/ I will confront them with the weeping of children/ The moans of the mothers and fathers/ The screams of the girls they raped/ Then poisoned and burnt/ They have made of me a shadow.../ But as a shadow I will haunt them day and night.*

She recites 'I Saw a Mountain', by Yiddish poet Moshe Shulstein, a pre-war colleague of Feder. She stands in front of a backdrop painting of a mountain of shoes. She wears a black gown, a striped cape and a prison-blouse with a yellow Star of David pinned to the chest.

Her arms reach out; her entire body is a gesture of longing: *'I saw a mountain higher than Mont Blanc/ And more sacred than Mount Sinai.../ In this world, this mountain stood/ Such a mountain I saw of shoes in Maidanek/ Hear! Hear the march/ Hear the shuffle of shoes left behind.../ Make way for the rows—for the pairs/ For the generations—for the years.../ The shoe army—it moves and moves.../ We are the shoes/ We are the last witnesses.*

Sonia Boszkowska was versed in a pre-war Yiddish song and theatre genre known as word concerts—solo performances devoted to the recital of literary works. She sings '*Eins, Zwei, Drei*', a song reflecting on life's fluctuating fortunes; and she is with the ensemble of *Der Goel,* The Redeemer, a play by Emil Bernhard, which Feder had directed in the Bunzlau concentration camp two years earlier.

Feder's one-act adaptation is set in the camp. It culminates in the prescient pre-war hymn '*Es Brent*', It's Burning, composed in 1938 by the carpenter songwriter Mordechai Gebirtig, who was shot four years later as he was marched from the Krakow Ghetto to the cattle wagons.

The song complements the play in its expression of anger at the townsfolks' passive reaction: *It's burning, brothers it's burning/ Our impoverished shtetl is burning/ Angry winds are blowing/ Breaking, burning and destroying/ And you stand and look on with folded arms/ And you stand and look on while our shtetl burns.*

The redeemer is unmasked; he is a false messiah. The townsfolk are angered and empowered. They know they must fend for themselves and answer the call to resistance: *Don't just stand there, brothers/ With your folded arms/ Don't just stand there, brothers/ Put out the fire...*

Sonia performs both pre-war Yiddish songs and a new generation of songs risen from the ashes. She sings a ballad that extolls the exploits of a partisan girl, written by the poet Hirsh

Glik in the Vilna Ghetto, barely two years earlier. *'Quiet, the night is full of stars/ And the frost is burning strong/ Remember how I once taught you/ To hold a gun in your hand.'*

Sonia is part of the ensemble that recreates a scene from the Bunzlau slave labour camp: Sami Feder and his comrades singing in the barracks late at night, to alleviate their suffering. A single candle lights the stage of the tent theatre as the performers now sing to depict their state of displacement.

And Sonia is part of the ensemble for the final song, the climax: *'Zog Nisht Keynmol',* Never Say, Hirsh Glik's partisan anthem: *Never say you are on your last way/ When blue skies are concealed by clouds of grey/ The hour we have longed for is surely near/ Beneath our tread the earth shall tremble: we are here!*

On the night of the premiere, the audience stood and sang the anthem with the performers. It was their collective moment. They were free to release their voices. It may have been the first time following the war that the partisan hymn was sung by the audience to conclude a memorial ritual. In years to come, it would become the standard.

The Kazet Theatre expanded its program. Feder added another two shows to its repertoire: the comedy, *'Zvei Hundert Toisent, der Groiser Gevins'*, Two Hundred Thousand, the Big Win, written by the most-loved of Yiddish writers Sholem Aleichem, and *'Der Farkishefter Schneider'*, The Bewitched Tailor, adapted by Feder from a Sholem Aleichem story.

The two plays were interwoven with popular pre-war songs and folk melodies. The scripts and sets appealed to audiences yearning for familiarity. Whereas the cabarets confronted the reality, the plays restored, for a moment, a sense of what once was. There is a Chagall-like magic in the backdrops of shtetl cottages, and a touch of modernity in the expressionist sets and costumes.

The troupe widened its reach, playing to patients in the camp hospital and at community events, including the opening of the Bergen-Belsen folk university. In the summer of 1947, they toured displaced persons camps in the British zone: Bad-Harzberg, Braunschweig and Hanover.

They were a band of troubadours on the road. Wherever they appeared, they were greeted by survivors who had recently emerged from their harrowing experiences. Whenever a scene was enacted, a tremor passed through the audience. This was a theatre of the unmasked. The performers' faces were naked in their expressions of grief, and enraged when depicting their tormentors.

In June 1947, the ensemble embarked on a tour of Belgium and France. The tour ended in Paris. Plans to tour London, New York, Buenos Aires and Palestine were never realised. The members of the troupe could not sustain the intensity. They wanted to move on and regain a sense of normalcy. In August 1947, the Kazet Theatre was disbanded, despite Sami Feder's efforts to keep it going.

Sonia and Sami settled in Paris. Sonia remained absorbed in theatre. She performed with the Parisian Yiddish Art Theatre. She studied humanities at the Sorbonne and moved in progressive circles. In later years, she spoke of her friendships with Edith

Piaf and Jean-Paul Sartre. It was one of her recurring stories, a rare display of pride and self-assertion. Beyond these brief mentions, concerning her life in Paris she said little.

In 1948, Sonia Boszkowska and composer-musician Henekh Kon toured a concert of Yiddish songs in France, Belgium, Switzerland and Germany. Henekh was a force in pre-war Yiddish cabaret and had worked with Sonia's mentor, Moshe Broderson. Henekh had fled his native Lodz and spent the war years in New York.

He met Sonia, in rehearsal, when he was commissioned to compose music for the Paris Yiddish Art Theatre. He was taken by her performance skills. He described her voice as a beautiful mezzo-soprano. He praised her instinctive sense of rhythm and the clarity of her tone. He composed songs for Sonia and accompanied her in acclaimed recitals in Paris.

Their first concert in Germany was in Bergen-Belsen. The last of the inmates were still waiting for visas elsewhere. Sonia was reunited with friends with whom she had shared the journey from terror to liberation. They embraced and wept and rejoiced in each other's presence. She was greeted with standing ovations and was mobbed by the audience.

While in Munich, Sonia and Henekh were invited to perform in displaced persons camps throughout Germany. After a concert for patients in a tuberculosis sanatorium, the audience poured out of the hall chanting: 'Bravo, Sonia! Bravo, Sonia!' People surrounded her car and pelted it with flowers.

As the car made its way from the sanatorium, Sonia sat lost in thought. The road to Munich wound through a valley, and the car was dwarfed by soaring peaks; the sun sank behind the mountains. The performance was over, replaced by a resonant silence.

In 1962 Sami and Sonia emigrated to Israel. The couple were farewelled in Paris at a banquet in Sami's honour. Journalists, performers and writers sang his praises. Their sojourn in Israel did not last long. The couple separated. Sami stayed in Israel. Sonia moved to New York. The move was abrupt, and final. Sonia never spoke of the reasons for the separation. She deflected my questions about Sami: 'He was once my husband. We worked in the Kazet Theatre. We performed together.' And again, weeks before she died, the blunt facts: 'Yes, I knew him. He was my husband.' That was all.

Her deflections were polite and detached. A dismissive wave of the hand, a sideways glance. And that gesture, the knuckles swiped over her closed eyes. It was Sonia's version of the art of the closed fist, but for an entirely different purpose: to defuse memory.

I listen to Sonia's album, *In Joy and Sorrow*, as I drive around the city: Sonia's Melbourne, the route she took on theatre outings with friends, from Joyce Street, left into St Kilda Street, past Ormond Park, and right into Glen Huntly Road. I stop at the traffic lights by the corner pub where, a decade earlier, I joined Sonia and Pinche for dinner on the eve of their move into aged care. There was no hint of regret that night. They could no longer live independently. That's the way it is. Let's get on with it.

I turn left and head towards the city on Brighton Road.

Darkness is falling. Sonia and her friends are buoyant in anticipation of a new play unfolding. Listening to the album, recorded in Tel Aviv in 1966, I am taken by the range of Sonia's voice and the drama she brings to her performance. Backed by an orchestra, she sings folksongs, love songs and ballads of longing.

There is one song that I play several times over as I approach the city's arts precinct—the concert halls and galleries that Sonia was drawn to. The riverbank cafes and restaurants bustle with life and movement. Crowds walk across Princes Bridge, to and from Flinders Street Station. The scene is at odds with the song: *'Einzam'*. Solitary, written by troubadour Itzik Manger, a balladeer of the people but also a loner. The lyrics express the deepest of human cravings: to be understood. '*No one knows what I say/ No one knows what I want.../ I put on my capulusz, and go on my way/ Where does one go late at night, in solitude, alone?*'

Einzam. Solitary. Perhaps this is what Sonia became after the loss of her loved ones. Certainly, this is what she is when she arrives in New York. She is forty years old, a single woman starting anew. She changes her name to Sonia Lizaron, combining the names of her mother and father, Liza and Aron, and will never again be Sonia Boszkowska.

Sonia cannot survive on singing alone. She puts on her hat and walks the avenues of New York clothed in a new identity, putting the past behind her, each step a testament to how far she has come from the day of her liberation. She learns a new trade and becomes a programmer at a time when computers are the size of a room. She lives in a fourth-floor walk-up apartment. She descends the stairs each morning, and sets out for work. In the evenings, she performs concerts or goes out with friends.

She is invited to sing in US cities and in Montreal and Toronto, and she embarks on tours: South America, Europe, Australia. Sonia is going solo, finding her own way. She becomes known in New York theatre circles and befriends writers and artists, including the author Isaac Bashevis Singer.

She once told me that she had observed Singer writing in his Manhattan apartment. He would randomly draw out cards from a filing system—on each card was the outline of a character—and he would bring them together in the one short story. Sonia's memories surfaced unexpectedly as passing comments, rearing up from and settling back to silence.

Who is Sonia in her silence? On stage, she embodied her people's suffering. But offstage she remains a mystery. Despite her efforts to forget the past, she is struggling with traumatic memories. She seeks ways to deal with the terror. This is something she was willing to speak of years later in the house in Joyce Street.

Her search had begun in Paris when, for a time, she became a follower of the teachings of Georges Gurdjieff. She was drawn to his 'system': an interweaving of music and movement as a means of releasing past trauma. She continued her practice in New York.

She travels to India and spends months in an ashram. She wakes pre-dawn and makes her way to the meditation hall. There are hundreds up at this hour, a community of seekers absorbed in their own thoughts, becalmed by the stillness of the hour. Sonia immerses herself in the daily routines. She is drawn to the scent of incense and the rhythms of the chants. She works in the ashram gardens, takes walks to the nearby village. She cherishes her solitude.

Meditation helps to temper the burden. She does not dwell on the past, and she no longer recounts her story, bar the odd reference and the recurring tales of Rossner, the man who saved her life, and of the bicycle trip through the camp to gather performers for the ensemble.

A curtain is being drawn, the horror confined to remembrance evenings. The stage is the one space where Sonia allows herself to revisit the past, but once the concert is over, that is the end of it. Shut out by that gesture—her knuckles brushed over her closed eyes, putting an end to painful memory.

Sometime in the 1980s, Sonia rekindled her friendship with Pinche Wiener. Sonia had first met the Wiener brothers, Pinche and Bono, in the Bund primary school she attended in Lodz. The brothers were daredevils back then. The tenement courtyards were their playgrounds. They made their way home from school over the rooftops to their third-floor apartment at 28 Szkolna Street. Their mother watched them anxiously as they clambered over the tiles towards the kitchen window.

The Wiener brothers were children of the Bund, and their parents, Moishe and Royze, like Sonia's, were party activists. The apartment was cluttered with books and pamphlets, and the nights were filled with friends engaged in fierce debate fuelled by vodka and whisky: a template many years later for gatherings at the Wiener brothers' house in Joyce Street.

Bono was born in Lodz in 1920. He changed his birthday to 5 May, the date of his liberation from Mauthausen slave labour camp in 1945. He was barely out of his teens when he became a leader of the Lodz ghetto resistance. He survived and became a builder of institutions and a co-founder of Melbourne's Holocaust Centre. He strode through life and the streets of the city, tall and proud. He looked at everyone he met with a disarming directness.

At community meetings and on memorial evenings he delivered fiery speeches. He founded a travel company so that he could visit his many pre-war friends in New York, Paris, Buenos Aires, Mexico City, Montreal—the many corners of the globe where they had settled.

In the Lodz ghetto, Bono was one of the keepers of a secret radio that was divided in two parts and hidden in two aluminium billies. Abram Goldberg took care of the other part. When the coast was clear, the parts were reconnected in the factory where both Abram and Bono worked. A foreman at the factory, Abram covered for Bono while he tuned in daily to the BBC and the Polish radio station *Swit*. Bono kept in contact with the Polish underground and government-in-exile, informing the inmates of the progress of the war, while lifting their morale with news of Allied victories.

The pair risked torture and execution; seventeen radio operators were arrested and shot at various times in the Lodz ghetto. Bono carried a cyanide tablet in his jacket should he be tortured for the names of resistance fighters.

Bono's parents died in the Lodz ghetto: Royze from illness,

Moishe from starvation. As a locksmith, Bono could have remained in Lodz after the ghetto was liquidated, but he chose to accompany his aunt Clara to Auschwitz. Clara perished there, and Bono resumed his resistance work, organising clandestine meetings in his barrack. When he received fifteen lashes for disobeying camp rules, he did not moan, but counted out each blow aloud, gaining the grudging admiration of the guard who whipped him.

He once told me he survived Auschwitz because, no matter what the circumstances, even on freezing winter nights after a day of slave labour, he washed himself; he traded a portion of his meagre rations for a piece of soap to preserve his dignity.

At his funeral, the mourners at his graveside farewelled him with 'An Oak Has Fallen', a song reserved for Bund heroes: *An oak has fallen, a fully grown oak, with a head higher than the oaks around it.* His portrait took pride of place on the dressing table in Sonia's room in the basement of the aged-care home.

Pinche was a different character. Restless. Nervous. Given to sudden outbursts of temper. After Poland was invaded, he served as a conscript in the Polish army. He endured the war years in the Soviet Union, partly as a slave labourer in the Arctic Circle, after a year spent in the city of Lvov as a captive of the Red Army, where he was locked in a cell with more than a hundred prisoners.

A small barred window, high on the wall, provided a glimpse of the sky. A drum served as a toilet. He was taken late at night to be interrogated. Always the same questions, night after night, under a single light globe and the sound of a tap dripping. His interrogators looked bored, sometimes threatening. They wanted him to confess to being a spy.

In later years, Pinche prided himself on his experiences: 'I may be an ignoramus in many things,' he said, 'but in two things I am a professor: in mud and hunger. And you can add lice—on this subject alone I have a doctorate.'

After the war, Pinche could not abide the sound of taps dripping. At the slightest hint, he changed the washers. He stocked many bars of soap and washed often, and he ate his meals with a feral vitality. He emerged from his ordeal embittered. 'Aron,' he would say to me. 'We thought we would save the world, and we proved to be idiots.'

The brothers were reunited in Lodz at war's end. They vowed never to separate. They fled Poland in 1948 through the Tatras Mountains to Czechoslovakia, made their way to Paris, and emigrated to Australia in 1950. After a stint as railway labourers in Perth and Adelaide, they settled in Melbourne.

Sonia began spending periods living with Pinche in the house on Joyce Street in the 1980s. She kept her apartment, dividing her time between Melbourne and New York, where she lived for six months each year. She climbed and descended the four flights of her New York walk-up until it was no longer physically possible. As always her decisions were calculated. She wound up her affairs in New York and moved in permanently with Pinche in Melbourne.

It was in the Wiener brothers' home that my friendship with Sonia flourished. After my son, Alexander, was born in 1993,

Sonia and Pinche became his surrogate grandparents. Alexander was drawn to Sonia's kindness and Pinche's mocking way: 'Your father is a no-good bastard,' he would say. Then, turning to me, 'Has he called you an idiot yet? Has he woken up to who you really are?'

Sonia and Pinche marked Alexander's height with a pencil on the kitchen door. It was a routine that concluded each visit. When Alexander developed a passion for Klezmer music and the clarinet, Sonia insisted on buying him a high-quality instrument. She came to the music store to choose it. She rang often, and when we did not answer, she left the same message: 'Well, let's hear some news.'

In her final years, Sonia's physical world narrowed, but she continued to move between Joyce Street and the Yiddish cultural centre, the Kadimah. She performed concerts for the elderly in the upstairs hall and on Wednesday mornings repaired and catalogued Yiddish books with volunteers in the ground-floor library. The books were dropped off by the sons and daughters of a passing generation. In this understated way, Sonia continued her commitment to cultural retrieval.

After she shifted into the aged-care home, she maintained the same steady pace. At first with Pinche, to and from the dining hall for meals and concerts. And then, after his death, to and from her room by the basement courtyard. Whenever I visited her, I walked the windowless corridor to the locked door and typed the code to be admitted.

'It should not be this way,' I think, when confronted by scenes of the infirm and demented living out their years in confined spaces. Over time I see the deterioration in some of the residents. I come to know those who wait in vain for visitors and those who pace the floors dishevelled, their dignity abandoned.

None of this seemed to concern Sonia. She kept her own counsel and protected her private space fiercely. When disoriented residents strayed into her room, she ordered them out. These were among the rare times I saw her flare up in anger. Her sharp command stopped them in their tracks; they did not dare come any further.

In the ghettos and camps, the boundaries between the private and public were non-existent: filth and wounds on display, indignities out in the open. There was nowhere to retreat to. In the displaced persons camps the lack of boundaries persisted; the inmates lived in close quarters. Only as they began to disperse were the boundaries re-established, as, one by one, alone or in couples, they peeled off and began new lives elsewhere.

In her final years, Sonia was forced to return to communal living. The boundaries were again being erased, but she knew how to handle them. She ate her meals seated with residents in the common dining room, kept to herself, and was done with it. Only when friends visited did her space expand. She wore make-up and was elegantly dressed, sitting bedside, or reclining on a sofa. Comfortable in her solitude. *Einzam.*

'How are you?' I ask, as I walk into the room.

'Hanging in there.'

~

How do we do justice to a life? The dead cannot speak for

themselves. Long after Sonia's death, it is a thought that haunts me. There are many gaps in Sonia's story, missing pieces. Who was she in the prime of her life? And in her partnership with Sami? How were they as a couple? What drove them apart? How did they appear to others who knew them?

In January 2017, I received an email from Arie Olewski. We had never met or been in contact. He lives in Herzliya, a coastal city north of Tel Aviv. He had read a tribute I had written to Sonia and he wished to publish it in a journal dedicated to the memory of Bergen-Belsen survivors. Arie and his sister Jochi knew Sonia and Sami as a couple, and knew them well.

'I grew up on their knees,' says Arie. 'They spent a lot of time in our home during their trips from Paris. But then Sonia vanished. I was about ten years old. I never saw her again.'

Arie was born in 1950 and Jochi in 1947. Sonia Boszkowska was their 'Aunt Sonia', he says, and Sami Feder, their 'Uncle Sami'. Arie's father, Rafael, was Sami's best friend. The men met in Bergen-Belsen. They were brothers in displacement. When the Kazet Theatre embarked on its European tour, Sami handed over his role as director of the camp's cultural department to Rafael.

'Do you know,' says Arie, 'that the camp functioned as an autonomous state? A kind of republic. And that under the noses of the British military it became a self-governing system that looked after its people?'

I am taken by the idea: a republic of the stateless. With its elected leaders, political parties and governing officials. And a citizenry composed of the displaced—the broken in body and the wounded in spirit.

In the first year after liberation, there were more than a thousand marriages, a response to the re-awakening of sexual desire and an urgent need for companionship. It was the main event, with up to fifty weddings a week. The grooms wore suits, and the brides wedding dresses, some made from parachutes. Apartment blocks were decorated and rations transformed into fine dishes. In that first year, there were more than five hundred births registered at the Bergen-Belsen hospital, and by 1948, more than a thousand.

'In this cynical world we live in, many people cannot understand what the camp provided,' says Arie. 'And the theatre played a big role in this. I am familiar with the reaction of the audience. It was a great deed that Sami performed at that time. He was the right person in the right place doing the right thing.

'My parents told me about the theatre when I was a young boy. They told me that Aunt Sonia was the leading performer and that Sami was the director. They told me everything, the good and the bad. I could not understand it all, but what they said made a lasting impression.'

I want to keep Arie talking. Now that I have found someone who knew Sonia and Sami I cannot let go. I probe, rephrase questions and seek new angles, trying to rekindle memory. 'My sister and I loved Uncle Sami and Aunt Sonia,' says Arie. 'And they loved us very much. We were the children they didn't have. They were always smiling. When they visited our apartment, they lit up when they saw us.

'In my child's eye I saw Sonia as stronger than Sami, more worldly. She was glamourous. She wore haute couture dresses, make-up and perfume. This is what has stayed with me most, her perfume. It was a part of who she was: a woman from abroad, a woman of Paris. She was passionate and dramatic, and very attractive. A *femme fatale*. I am sure many men were drawn to her.

'Something was not quite right between them. They were very unhappy in Paris. Sami was a dreamer. He lived for his art, and he lived in the past. He was frustrated in his efforts to make a living from theatre. I have letters Sami wrote to my father from Paris. Sami complains that he and Sonia are poor. He needs money.

'They lived like dogs in Paris. There was talk of a small business, a shop they ran together. The business struggled. Sami was a *schlimazl* with money. They finally left and settled in Israel for a short while. Then one day Sonia disappeared from our life.

'Sami spent much of his time writing his memoirs and histories of the theatre. He needed money to have them printed. He asked for help from people he once knew in Bergen-Belsen. He was always looking for a publisher and receiving rejections. He remarried. His second wife, Dwora, was a lovely woman, but they never had children.

'Then a few years ago I heard that Sonia was living in Australia. I thought, this is fantastic. I wanted to hear from her again. I wanted to see her again, but it was too late. She died before I could get in touch. Sami died in 2000. They are all gone now: my father and mother, and the citizens of Bergen-Belsen. Your tribute has brought back many memories.

I phone Arie's sister, Jochi. Her voice is strong and she is forthright in her views. Even over such a distance I can tell she is tough and grounded. 'Listen, I can tell you something,' she says. 'As I speak I see Sonia in front of me. She had big eyes. She wore bright red lipstick. She was very particular in her make-up. She was a person who took care of herself. She was always perfectly dressed, and she was very kind. I would say, gentle. She never lost her temper, but she was in charge, and Sami was a shadow in her presence.

'He adored her. His life revolved around her. He was nervous. Listen, I speak to you and I see him. He was jumpy, and his hands were always moving. He was a kind soul, but he was choking her with love. He worshipped her and was unsure of himself in her company. Sonia was self-contained. She had an aura about her. I am sure she knew what she was doing, and I am sure she initiated the separation. After they parted, I never saw her again.'

I am surprised by what Ari and Jochi have told me. I had always imagined Sami as the assertive one, and Sonia as living and performing beside a dominant man. I had deduced this, in part, from photos of Sonia and Sami separately and as a couple in the displaced persons camp and in post-war Paris.

In several photos, Sami wears a dark suit and tie and a white shirt. His features are sharp: deeply set eyes, receding black hair combed back from his forehead. His expression is thoughtful. He emanates authority and appears aware of the image he is projecting.

I had also assumed Sami was the dominant one in the

partnership from what I observed in Sonia's final years with Pinche. He was loving, but he often belittled her opinion and berated her for forgetfulness. When we visited the aged-care home, Sonia would get vodka from the fridge and bowls of almonds and fruit and slices of orange cake, and then say little. She appeared resigned, and compliant.

There were times when I saw her flinch at Pinche's outbursts, and then become silent. She would shrug and close her eyes, and when she opened them her expression would be restored to neutral. Yet there was also the easy harmony of a couple familiar with each other's ways, and a kind of love between them born of their common youth as children of the Bund and a mutual love of Lodz, their childhood city.

Pinche's nostalgia for Lodz remained till the end. I visited him on the final night of his life, as he lay in his hospital bed. 'Lodz was a dirty, polluted city,' he said, in the pugnacious tone I knew so well. As always, his defiance was tempered by a sense of wonder. I had seen it many times over the years, his rapid switches from belligerence to wonder.

'Yes, Lodz was a dirty polluted city,' he repeated. 'But it was *my* city, and it was my home, and it was the home of my *mamushka* and *tatushka*.' These were the last words I heard Pinche say. He died hours later.

After Pinche's death Sonia pared her life back to essentials. Among the few possessions she retained were the photo of proud Bono and one of her mother and father and her brother taken before the war in that dirty, polluted city. But she kept no trace of Sami or the Kazet Theatre. No photos of Paris or New York, or her walk-up apartment. Nothing from that long stretch of life between her childhood and youth in Poland and her present life, bar the painted portraits, the album cover, and the family photos taken in Lodz, her true home, despite it all.

I review the photos I have of Sonia and Sami. In one, taken in Paris in 1947, they are seated in the restaurant of the Sarah Bernhardt theatre. There's a bottle of champagne on the table in front of them, a second bottle rests in a silver bucket. Perhaps the photo was taken after a performance of the Kazet Theatre on the last leg of its European tour. It may have been after the theatre's final appearance.

In the light of my conversations with Arie and Jochi, I detect the beginnings of a shift in Sami's appearance. He is showing signs of ageing. He was considerably older than Sonia. She is in her prime, glowing. He appears uncertain. Perhaps I am reading too much into it. 'Who knows what goes on in a marriage?' says Jochi. 'We were children who did not have grandparents. Arie and I loved them both. We needed them as much as they needed us.

'Listen, my mother lost everyone. She had a brother who was a prisoner in Auschwitz. He was a member of the Sonderkammando work units, one of the men who were forced to dispose of the bodies from the gas chambers. What he saw no human being should have to see. Any dissent meant instant death.'

Jochi's uncle took part in the revolt of the Sonderkammando on 7 October 1944. The plan was to destroy the gas chambers, inspire an uprising, and make a run for it. The men hoarded gunpowder smuggled in by women enslaved at a nearby munitions factory, and prepared grenades with which to blow up the crematoria. They attacked the SS and Kapos with hammers, two machine guns, stones, knives and axes, and they partly destroyed Crematorium 4. 'My mother's brother was killed for it,' says Jochi.

'My father had one brother left, a rabbi in Brooklyn. This was all we had, and he was far away. We didn't see him often. The friends my parents made in Bergen-Belsen became our family. They went through the fire together, but each one was different.

'You know, my father talked about the past, and he wrote about the past, but I don't think he lived in the past. He felt obliged to remember and record it. And he did this so that what happened would be honoured, and what he had seen never forgotten.

'But Sami lived in the past. That was the difference. Sami was obsessed. And yes, his hands were always moving, in a restless way. Listen, I talk to you and again I see him in front of me, his curly hair and his fading looks. I see him sitting next to Sonia, and I see how anxious he was.'

Of the day that British troops liberated Bergen-Belsen, Sami writes: 'We were freed, but we were not free.' Decades later he is still not free. He is weighed down by the memory. He remains an inmate of the republic of the stateless. Bergen-Belsen is now overgrown with grass, he laments. The mass graves are sinking beneath a newly planted forest.

Among the buried is his sister, Fela, who perished in the

camp. Her photo appears in his memoirs. She wears a dark scarf and a checked shirt, and she looks directly at the camera. The image has a haunting aura, perhaps due to the viewer's knowledge of her fate. Sami is driven to resurrect her, and document all that he witnessed. He cannot unsee it.

The literal translation of the Yiddish title of Sami's camp memoir is: *Through Twelve Fires of Hell.* It is an apt title. The memoir burns with the horror of his experience, and his resolve. He does not flinch in the telling. He depicts the depths of human depravity in accounts that trace the descent of the victims into their private hells and the strategies they employed to survive and evade their captors' attentions.

Sami's forays into the fires of hell begin early. He has his first inklings in 1925, in Frankfurt Am Main. He is nineteen years old. Every night, on his way home from the acting school, he passes a shopfront displaying anti-Semitic books, woodcut caricatures and copies of the Nazi publication *Der Sturmer.* His people are depicted as an avaricious race of perverts and vermin. They are the root cause of Germany's woes, parasites to be exterminated. Sami is enraged and drawn to political action.

In Berlin, he witnesses Hitler's ascent to power: goose-stepping thugs on the march, demonstrations, random beatings. After the burning, in February 1933, of the Reichstag, the Nazis round-up socialists, communists and stateless Jews, and deport them to the first concentration camps: Dachau and Oranienberg. As a journalist and theatre director, and a Jewish non-citizen active in progressive circles, Sami Feder is high on the blacklist.

One day, while he is at work typesetting the *Encyclopaedia*

Judaica in German translation, he receives word from his landlady. His room had been ransacked by the criminal police and the SS. They had taken his typewriter, photos and camera, manuscripts and papers. They were waiting for him.

Sami makes his way to the home of a friend—a member of a socialist youth group, a printer and workmate. After a week in hiding, he steals back to his room and gathers a few possessions. There is a letter on his desk, left for him by the police, warning him that he has forty-eight hours to leave Germany or face dire consequences. The time limit has long expired.

Sami is smuggled out of Berlin to a nearby town, where he boards an express train heading southeast to the Polish border. He is arrested by the SS at Breslau Station, imprisoned and interrogated. They demand he tell them where and with whom he has spent the twelve days since he was ordered to leave Germany. Drawing on his acting skills, Sami insists he is a naïve young man who is anxious to return to Poland to reunite with his family. After paying a bribe in jewellery, he is handcuffed and taken to the station, locked in a compartment and deported to Poland.

On his arrival at Katowice Station, he is arrested for not possessing a Polish passport, and shunted back in a locked compartment to Germany. He steals back into Poland by merging with a group of German Catholics who cross the border to pray in a Polish church on Sunday mornings. Assuming guises is Sami's profession, and a bag containing the bare necessities is his most trusted companion.

After a short stay in his mother's house, Sami heads for the epicentre of Yiddish life, Warsaw. He goes to the artists' union and to the Yiddish Writers Club, at the legendary address: Tlomackie 13. He climbs the well-worn stairs to the clubrooms and offices. He talks with authors and journalists and is inducted as a guest member, but his warnings of the perils posed by the ascent of Hitler fall on deaf ears. The establishment is complacent. This is nothing new, they say. You are over-anxious. Pogroms come and go. We know how to handle it. In Warsaw, we are free to go about our business.

Sami is in despair. He is Nietzsche's madman, clutching a lantern on a summer morning, dashing through the marketplace among the self-assured and the unbelieving, proclaiming: 'Wake up! Prepare! This is a danger of a different order!' Sami *is* prepared. He is one of the first to have witnessed the Nazi party's power, and among the first to understand what it portended.

When Sami and Sonia meet again in Bergen-Belsen they had both journeyed through those fires of hell. Sonia is a partner in Sami's mission and active in creating the theatre within weeks of their liberation. At some point, they become a couple.

Perhaps it began during the time of their collaborations in Benzin before the war. Perhaps they were one of the many couples who would stroll through the forest in the displaced persons camp grounds, a favoured place for secret trysts and sexual encounters. Or perhaps they fell in love on tour in Brussels and Antwerp. There are photos of the couple at that time in which they appear radiant.

Fate is fragile. This story is fragile. Arie Olewski emails me a scanned copy of the two sides of a flimsy sheet of hotel stationery, dated 1960. The paper is razor thin. The sheet is headed: 'The Sharon Hotel in Herzliya by the Sea', evoking blue skies, ocean breezes and the waters of the Mediterranean. Glowing sands and crowded beaches, open-necked shirts and summer dresses. The sheet is filled with messages addressed to Sonia in Paris.

Both sides of the sheet are filled with greetings written in fountain pen. Every bit of space is taken. Some messages are scrawled vertically, others horizontally. Some are written on a diagonal, or squeezed into the corners. The messages were gathered at a reunion of the Bergen-Belsen Association, and written by ex-citizens of the republic of the stateless. Among them former members of the Kazet Theatre. They are more than citizens. They are comrades, brothers and sisters, but Sonia was not with them. I don't know why she did not join them, but it is clear from the messages that her friends missed her.

Their sentiments are recorded in Yiddish, French, Russian and Polish. The republic was host to many languages. The ex-citizens have resettled, but the republic maintains its hold. They ache for Sonia's presence.

'Sonia, where are you?' 'My dear Sonitchka, all your friends are meeting. It's such a pity that you are not with us! All our thoughts are with you.' 'Sonia, I hope you have remembered how we ate together in Paris.' 'Dear Sonia! Greetings to you. I regret that I have not seen you since the war. Remember me.'

'Dear Sonia, I am sorry you are not among us. Greetings and kisses.' 'We would dearly love to see you.' 'We hope that you will shortly come to stay permanently.' And the message which cuts deepest: 'It is strange to see Sami without you.'

Something is amiss. Sami writes: 'Dear Sonitchka, I send you my most heartfelt greetings.' Sami is present with former members of the theatre, but his partner is absent.

Sami is not able to fully return to civilian life. He was of one time and one place, a time that encompassed many places, way-stops in hell. He found his strength in hell, but once his ordeal was over, and he was in his promised land, he still felt stateless. Years later, Jochi articulates it. 'He did not have roots in the present. He remarried, but he never got over Sonia. Listen. I can tell you something. Sonia and Sami's great love was of a certain time and circumstance.'

Jochi is a daughter of Bergen-Belsen, conceived and born in the republic of the stateless. 'Listen. I can tell you something,' she repeats. 'Sami and Sonia created something out of nothing. They came together, and they did amazing things. They climbed to a great height. For a moment, they stood at the summit, but there was nowhere higher to go. They could not adjust to a new reality. In Paris, Sami became a fallen hero, but a hero he remained.'

Jochi has led me to the irony. For years, Sami was ahead of history. He led the way, and he lit the way. He lifted spirits. He saved lives, and provided comfort. Then history overtook him. The price he paid was immense. He lost Sonia.

Yet, he attained something else. He took on the role of witness, the chronicler. There is a photo of Sami in later years, seated at a writing desk. He is surrounded by papers, books and documents, at work on his memoirs and histories. His writing is driven by a burning need to preserve all of it: the reviews, journal articles, newspaper reports, scripts, sheet music, eyewitness accounts and testimonies. Every scrap of information.

Sami writes with a sense of immediacy. He recalls both the horror and the moments of reprieve. He is fully present to the past, resuming yet another retelling of his life story. He is Dante's Virgil, a guide in the Inferno. *Abandon hope all ye who enter here*, reads the infamous inscription, but Sami Feder is not dealing in allegory. He takes his readers into a literal hell. He descends again and again into the underworld.

But he does not write of abandoned hope. That would be a betrayal of those who returned to the world of the living. And he does not offer false hope. That would be a betrayal to those who perished. Sami simply holds the lamp, descends, shines the light in the darkest corners. And returns with the story.

There is one tale that recurs several times. It is the go-to story, emblematic, recited to journalists and visiting dignitaries: One day, in mid-1945, an inmate of the displaced persons camp makes his way to the rooms of the Kazet Theatre. There is a girl in a nearby camp reserved for former Polish prisoners, he says, who wishes to transfer to a Jewish camp. She had survived on Aryan papers, and has all but forgotten the Yiddish language. The ensemble takes on her case and she is brought to Bergen-Belsen.

This is the tale she tells them. When the war broke out the girl was eleven years old. She made her way with her mother and father, brother and sister, from their native village to Warsaw where they lived until January 1942. As the net tightened, they fled Warsaw and hid in a hamlet on the outskirts of Lublin in Eastern

Poland. With her Aryan looks, the girl was assigned the task of scavenging for food and water.

Returning to the hiding place after an outing, she discovered that while she was away the SS had rounded up her family. Her mother, sister and young brother had been shot alongside other Jews who were hiding in the village, and her father deported to Treblinka death camp.

The girl fled the hideout and wandered day and night over field and forest, and from village to village, in dread of capture. After she had wandered for months, a farmer had pity on her and took her in as a shepherd. One afternoon, while at work in the pastures, she was overcome by a deep longing. She wept and, without thinking, she began singing the Yiddish songs her mother and father had taught her.

As she sang, she did not notice a Polish boy hidden behind a tree. He heard her singing and betrayed her to the Gestapo. She was arrested, interrogated and beaten, and given five minutes to admit she was Jewish. If she confessed, they said they would not harm her. If she did not confess, they would shoot her. She remained silent.

The two interrogators raised their guns and told her to walk. They directed her to a forest. On the way, they met an old German man. The officers told him what they were doing. He lifted his hand and said, let her go. She will not survive long. What harm can it do? Let her live a few more days. The officers told her to run.

When she was out of sight, she rubbed her hands together and pressed them to her cheeks. Had she been shot? Was she alive? Suddenly she saw the boy who betrayed her. She wanted to gouge out his eyes so that he would never betray anyone again. The boy sank to his knees. He crossed himself over and over and begged her to forgive him. In return he hid her and brought her food. They became close friends.

One day the boy told her that a battalion of German soldiers had arrived in the nearby village and was looking for Jews. You must leave, he said, or you will be caught and shot. She was paralysed with terror. She asked him, how can I escape when I have no identity papers? The boy left and returned an hour later with bread and salami and papers he had stolen from a village girl. She wept, then kissed him and left.

She roamed the countryside for three years disguised as a Polish girl. She was chased and held up, searched and interrogated. She was prized property; handing in a Jewish girl to the Gestapo earned you a kilo of sugar. She was finally arrested in a village. She showed the soldiers the papers the boy had stolen; the documents saved her life. But she was deported to a slave labour camp in Germany, where she was liberated by the Americans and placed in a displaced persons camp reserved for former Polish prisoners.

She did not know if any Jews were alive. She was told they had all been sent to Auschwitz and gassed. She contemplated suicide. Why live if my people have not survived? One fine day a man arrived in the camp in search of relatives. She recognised him and wept for joy. She could barely speak. He arranged everything, and brought her to Bergen-Belsen.

The girl's name was Mala Friedman. She joined the theatre

and relearnt the Yiddish she had all but forgotten. She embraced the ensemble as family, and they embraced her. She became one of their lead performers.

There is a story that appears in Sami's memoir *With Clenched Fists*, and again in *Through Twelve Fires of Hell*, a second volume of memoirs written when Feder was almost eighty. Many years had gone by, and still, he was not done with it. I assume he wrote them in his apartment in Herzliya. Perhaps, when he lifted his head, he had a view of the sea through a window. If so, I doubt whether he dwelt on it.

His mind is in Bergen-Belsen on a cold evening, in the first winter after liberation. The windows twinkle with frost and the trees are coated in ice. The wind whistles in the chimneys. The stove glows red, and the freshly cut wood crackles. Sami sits by the stove reading a book.

A light knock on the door interrupts his reading. The door slowly opens and a woman enters. It is difficult to tell how old she is. At one moment, she appears to be young. A moment later her eyes are overcome by fatigue and a profound sadness.

She pauses by the open door, stares at Sami and says: 'Forgive me. Perhaps I am disturbing you.' She is unable to say more. Tears fill her eyes. Her lips are trembling.

'Sit down,' Sami says. 'Warm yourself. Calm down. Perhaps I can help?'

Slowly she sits, then suddenly she springs back up. She covers her face with her hands and, as if speaking to herself, she says, 'No! No one can help me!'

She sits back down and, in a near-whisper, begins to recount her tale.

'I was born in Hungary. My parents were orthodox Jews and wealthy merchants. I was their only daughter. I studied medicine and worked as a doctor. Then the Germans invaded. Concentration camp…As a doctor specialising in women's health, I was assigned to the women's sick bay. My god! Why did I ever become a doctor?'

She falls silent and surveys her surroundings. She glances at the door and makes a move towards leaving.

'Perhaps you will have something to drink,' Sami suggests.

She glances at Sami, shakes her head, and continues. 'I don't know if you are aware that pregnant women were sent straight to the gas chambers. Many women tried to hide their pregnancies. They often fainted at their work place. Some of the pregnant women were brought by their friends to me in the sickbay. They kissed my hands and begged me to save them. But how? It was forbidden to give birth in the camps. Every one of them pleaded: "Save me. I am still so young. Please, help me." Their pleas cut into my heart. My God!'

She pauses and remains silent for several minutes, then exclaims, 'Is there a God? Where is he? Where are my grandfathers, and where are the rabbis? Where are our prophets? Where is the Messiah? If there is no Jewish Messiah, where is the Christian Messiah? He preached love of man for man. Where is that man? Does humanity exist?

'"How can I help you?" I asked the women. I told them, "If you wish to live, your child cannot be allowed to live."

'One woman looked at me in terror. She did not dare weep aloud. She whimpered and moaned like a wounded animal, and bit her lips till they bled. As her moaning grew louder, I bound her mouth with a kerchief so that the SS men standing by the window would not hear her.

'These two hands! With these two hands I strangled her baby; but at the last moment, the mother ripped off the kerchief from her mouth and screamed: "Murderer! Give me back my child."

'I was covered in sweat. With my last ounce of strength, I held my hands to her mouth. She bit my hand until it bled and began weeping. I gave her an injection and she fell asleep. I packed the foetus in paper and hid it behind the barrack. The mother was saved, but for how long?

'Thus I strangled babies. Me? With my own hands? God, why did you choose me to murder unborn children? Now they are all dead. Why did you let me live? No. They are not dead. I see them everywhere. Wherever I go, wherever I stand, I see them, by day and by night. I cannot sleep or rest. I did not even allow them their first cry. Me. Me.

'And now I hear them cry. All of them. They chase and pursue me. I can no longer be a doctor. My dream was to help people, to hear the first cry of a newborn baby and to witness the joyous smile of the mother, and now I am terrified. I do not trust my own hands. To save the mothers, I had to murder their babies.'

The woman cries out. 'Forgive me for telling you this,' she says. 'Perhaps it will make me feel a little lighter.'

Quietly, she weeps. Sami remains silent. At that very moment, as if to mock them, a newborn child can be heard crying in the room next door. The woman leaps up. She holds her hands to her head, places them over her ears and runs from the room in terror. A cutting wind bursts into the room. Sami steps out, but the woman has vanished.

On Friday, 19 September 1986, fifty-one-year-old Chaim Orlin entered the offices of the Netherlands Institute for War Documentation carrying a large photograph album. He had long intended, he explained, to entrust the photographic collection to an archive. He lived in Amsterdam, and the institute was internationally renowned for its collection of archives concerning World War II and its aftermath.

Chaim felt a sense of urgency. In his haste, he offered few details in handing over the album. He mentioned only that his sister, Cecillia 'Zippy' Orlin, had compiled it from photographs taken during the period when Bergen-Belsen was a displaced persons camp for survivors. With that, he left the premises.

The album weighed fifteen kilograms. There were 1117 photos, many with brief captions: Chaim's gift was the most complete photographic record of life in the camp.

Historians Erik Somers and Rene Kok, who worked at the institute, wanted to know more about the album. Who was Zippy Orlin? Who had taken the photos? How did they end up in the Netherlands? Chaim would know.

Four days after receiving the album, they attempted to contact him. To their dismay, they learned that Chaim had died in his sleep the night before. It took them years to track down the answers, which they published in the 1998 yearbook of the institute. Soon after, Somers and Kok wrote a book about the album, and of the woman who compiled it.

Cecillia 'Zippy' Orlin was born in 1922 to an impoverished family in the town of Siesiekeij, Lithuania. She was the second of five children. Her father, Yisrael Orlin, struggled to support them. In 1928, Yisrael's brother, who had emigrated to South Africa, convinced him and his family to join him. Yisrael earned a living peddling fresh produce from a horse and cart in Johannesburg. He worked his way to buying a truck and built a thriving business.

Zippy spent the war years as a secretary of the South African Jewish Board of Deputies. Early in 1946, the board invited Zippy, then twenty-four, to work as a volunteer in the Bergen-Belsen displaced persons camp. Her fluency in Yiddish, they assumed, would make up for her inexperience in relief work.

After a farewell banquet in the Carlton Hotel in Johannesburg, Zippy left for Paris where she was inducted into the work. She arrived by army truck in Bergen-Belsen in July. As the truck jolted over a dusty corrugated road, the driver, a former prisoner, told her that many inmates were marched along this road to their deaths. The camp population had swelled to ten thousand with the influx of Jews fleeing a resurgence of anti-Semitic violence in their former home towns in Eastern Europe.

Throughout her stay, Zippy was acutely conscious of the historic moment. She documented her experiences in photos. She took some herself, but most were taken by friends and co-workers, 'Willy with the Leica', and Harry Koop, both members of the transport unit. Zippy also collected photos taken before her time, of scenes that confronted the British soldiers when the Bergen-Belsen transit camp was liberated.

Zippy worked in the displaced persons camp for twenty-seven months, and left when the population was rapidly dwindling. On her return to South Africa in 1949, she wrote a short account of her experiences and began work on the album. She took the photos with her to London, where she trained as a beautician specialising in facial massage, and to Tel Aviv, where she settled in 1960. She spent her final months in Johannesburg and died there in 1980, of cancer. After her death, her brother Chaim found the album among her personal possessions.

The photos provide a detailed record of daily life in the de facto republic of the stateless. Though there appear to be no photos of Sami and Sonia, the pictures were taken when they were there. They depict the camp as they would have seen it.

Some of the images document Zippy's assignments. She conducted an exercise club for young women, and she worked alongside the camp hospital nurses. She taught at the elementary school, and looked after a group of orphans. She accompanied children who had tuberculosis to sanatoriums in Italy and Switzerland.

She attended births and circumcisions, weddings, concerts, dances and parties. In the photos, she appears light and unburdened, as if on an adventure, thriving because she is striking out on her own, independent of family. She is pictured standing with groups of children, her hands resting on their shoulders. She is smartly dressed, and her hair is swept up in a beehive.

Zippy is both participant and observer, empathetic but free of the trauma. Perhaps this is the reason why, of all those who worked and lived in the camp, it was she who assembled the most complete photographic record. Her captions are haiku-like poems of remembrance.

Of a photo of corpses lined up on the verge beside a road on the day of liberation, Zippy writes: 'They are no more. The road to death for 30,000.' Of a panoramic view of the displaced persons camp she observes: '1945. The SS torturers move out and the tortured remnants move in.' Of the tombstones erected where the barracks once stood: 'Amongst the rubble a tree now grows, that we shall remember Jews, Christians. The known and the unknown.'

Of the camp survivors: 'They wanted to live, to provide, to be a child, to play, to keep law and order, to feast, to celebrate and to care for soul and body.' Of the children's choirs and theatre performances: 'Acting and singing gave expression to their regained lust for life.'

A photo of infants at play is captioned: 'Sturdy little toddlers romped in the flower-covered fields and expressed the childish emotions so long suppressed.' And of two young children about to leave the camp, Zippy writes: 'With heads held high they faced the future.'

There are photos of the camp hospital where Sonia went from bed to bed collecting testimonies. We see doctors and nurses tending patients, clinics for babies, and camp residents riding bicycles, and a battalion of Jewish-inmate appointed policemen, dressed in uniforms and black berets, standing at attention.

Camp leaders sit at meetings and conduct press conferences. They attend congresses of the liberated. The inmates take part in election campaigns. They ride trucks displaying banners and posters of candidates. They hand out leaflets, and line up to cast their votes for members of the Central Committee.

We see the inmates practising trades in vocational schools and workshops—bricklaying, welding, lathe work, dress designing and dressmaking. We see weddings: the men wear suits and ties, and the women, festive dresses. Young men and women attend parties. They wear party hats; the wine and beer is flowing. There is a photo of typesetters composing the Yiddish script of the camp newspaper, *Unzer Shtimme*, *Our Voice*, and of the co-editor, Arie and Jochi's father, Rafael Olewski, reading an edition.

There are many photos of children. More than two thousand lived in the camp: a thousand were born there, and more than five hundred orphaned children were brought there from all over Europe. Dressed in light summer clothes, or swathed in hooded winter coats and jackets, they clutch dolls and toy animals. Some are pictured with doctors holding stethoscopes to their hollow chests. They wear sturdy boots and ride scooters. They cook and gather wood and walk hand in hand with their teachers and childcare workers.

Young children exercise in the fields in summer; they are lean, their rib cages protruding. Their backs are arched, heads tilted back, and their chests pushed forward. Their upper bodies are bathed in sunlight. The children are restored before our eyes from gaunt loners to potential wholeness. There are children watched over by teachers and nurses and doted on by their parents, in kindergartens, primary and junior high schools; the children perform gymnastics and eat at communal breakfasts.

Babies and toddlers are paraded in prams and strollers by young mothers. The women's faces and the building behind them are lit by the sun. The predominant expression is of proud defiance. They seem to be saying: Despite it all, we have returned to life, and are savouring each moment—the open skies, the chestnut trees in the courtyards, the rustle of leaves as we stroll the camp grounds. Our bodies are restored. We have given birth. We breastfeed our babies. We are mothers. Lovers. Workers. We are women.

There is just one photo of the Kazet Theatre, taken on 15 April 1946, a year after the liberation, and three months before Zippy arrived in the camp. The performers parade through the streets. Sonia and Sami are most likely there, perhaps in the front row, obscured by the theatre banner.

The group is not captioned as the Kazet Theatre, but as displaced persons marching to the site of Camp 1, the Horror Camp. The cordoned-off grounds were open for the occasion. A stone had been erected in honour of those who lay there, buried in the weeks after liberation. The march commemorates the unveiling of the monument.

Those carrying the banner wear concentration camp uniforms. The men filing behind them are dressed in suits and open-necked white shirts, and the women in jackets, skirts and blouses. They look directly at the camera, conscious of the significance of the occasion; their expressions are grim and determined.

They are engaged in a political act—a deliberate return to the site of their enslavement. They reflect the sentiments expressed in the first verse, and the final stanza, of the Partisan Hymn, with which they concluded the memorial service: *The hour we have longed for is surely near. Beneath our tread the earth shall tremble: we are here!*

The photos project action and busy-ness. They capture life returning: the fragile balance between rebirth and unbearable memory. The displaced persons camp is a republic of survivors hungry to resume living; and they are proud. There may be British troops who appear to be in control, relief workers from outside agencies and organisations, serving their needs, but the de facto republic is run by the inmates. They crave agency. They are taking control of their lives and asserting authority. They call themselves *Sh'erit ha-Pletah*, a biblical term, 'the saved remnant'. They are rebuilding their lives and the lives of their people.

And we see the beginnings of the dismantling of the republic, photos of inmates at farewell parties at which, Zippy observes, 'joy and sadness mingled'; and of inmates in the act of leaving, lugging suitcases, boarding trucks, standing on railway platforms. Waving farewell to those yet to receive the required papers. The carriages pull out of the station, departing for distant places. Bergen-Belsen is fading from sight, a smudge on a receding horizon.

Yet, there are limits. The photos don't convey the inner turmoil: the inmates' fear of sleep and the disturbing dreams that waited to ambush them; the hours, lying awake, waiting for the dawn to deliver them from memory and the nights of crippling aloneness.

They do not convey the alienation, the acute suspicion of outsiders, and the fits of violence and rage that could erupt at any time, triggered by a trivial remark or an official barking an order, or the panic evoked by the sight of uniformed soldiers.

They do not depict the obsessive hoarding of food by inmates fearful of renewed hunger, or the physical wounds that prevented some women from bearing children, or the emotional scars that had broken some of the inmates' capacity for intimacy. They do not capture the cynicism of children, old before their time, their loss of trust and their suspicion.

They do not show the inmates who wandered about insane, eyes vacant, or the former slaves who panicked at the thought of labour. They do not capture the erratic shifts: the euphoria of freedom, shattered a moment later by the unbidden pain of loss and horror. And they do not portray the thirst for vengeance, brought to light in the poems and songs collected by Sami and Sonia and their comrades.

Nor do they capture the manic search for loved ones: inmates scouring Red Cross lists, and camp lists in the frantic hope of finding a familiar name; the men and women going from block to block, knocking on doors, in search of a lost son, a daughter, a wife or husband; or the dashed illusion that the person walking ahead may be, dare I believe it, a missing parent, a sibling?

And they cannot portray the endless days, the monotony, the cramped living spaces, the morbid fear of contagion and the sense of being hemmed in—hemmed in by walls and barbed-wire fences, by remembrance, and by interminable waiting. Waiting for the future. Waiting for admission into the family of nations. Waiting to be finally done with statelessness.

Sami observes in his memoirs: 'The British officers who liberated us wear a sympathetic expression, but they are condescending. They pity us, but material assistance is slow in coming.' There are food shortages; inmates steal from the camp to augment rations. They catch hares and trade cigarettes for food with local farmers. There is a rampant black market.

There are no-go zones, restrictions on movement. Officers' quarters have signs warning that beyond a certain point unauthorised intruders will be arrested; there are tensions with the British military authorities who retain control of security and with members of the United Nations Relief and Rehabilitation Agency, who are now in charge of camp administration.

And there are times when the gates of the camp are locked and the perimeters patrolled by armed soldiers. Movement in and out of the camp is strictly regulated. Locked gates trigger panic: shortness of breath, cold sweats, uncontrollable weeping and the bitter sense that despite all that they had endured, the inmates' ordeal is far from over.

On 29 May 1946, the gates are locked, and a twenty-four-hour curfew is imposed on the camp inmates. The Jewish Central Committee declares a general strike. Four thousand protestors mass in Freedom Square. Placards proclaim: 'Enough of concentration camp', 'Away with the wire', 'We will not allow ourselves to be imprisoned in camp', 'Open the Gates of Belsen'.

Sami Feder and Rafael Olewski are two of the speakers on the podium. Their speeches voicing the inmates' grievances are met with cries of anger. The inmates are incensed by the closure of the gates. They are outraged that they are being collectively punished for security breaches committed by other camp residents. They demand to be officially identified as Jews, and accorded the same rights as the citizens of other nations held in Bergen-Belsen.

The demonstrators march through the camp. The procession stretches for hundreds of metres. There are women wheeling babies and infants in strollers, school children and youths and camp inmates who have until now remained neutral.

Two hundred metres from the main gate, the marchers are confronted by British officers who advise them to elect a delegation to represent them. Sami Feder and Rafael Olewski are among the four men chosen to negotiate with the camp authorities. They leave the camp escorted by the officers.

An hour passes with no sign of their return. The demonstrators are restless. They inch towards the camp gate, despite the efforts of their own Jewish police to keep order. On the other side of the fence there are British soldiers dressed in riot gear, guns drawn, water cannon at the ready. The delegation returns, accompanied by the UN relief agency's chief and the camp's military commander. Their speeches are placatory but contain no concrete promises.

The protestors are incensed. It can be seen in the photos. The inmates are tough and alert one year after liberation. Some break from the assembled crowd and surge towards the gate.

They tear at the barbed-wire fences. The soldiers drench them with water. Camp guards hurl stones and slabs of timber. A band of former partisans cut the water hoses.

The battle between the liberators and the liberated continues for twenty-five minutes. Then the protestors hack the gate open. 'Go ahead, shoot if you dare!' they jeer, as they swarm through, and march on the perimeter road, triumphant.

The cordon of soldiers is removed, and the curfew lifted. Some services are improved. The inmates' movement in and out of the camp is less restricted, and a new UN administrator is appointed, one far more attuned to the inmates' desire for autonomy. But they remain stranded, caught between countries they can no longer return to and a world reluctant to take them in. They are liberated, but they are not yet free. Still, they must wait.

On 11 June 1947, after a year of negotiations, delays, false starts and setbacks, and finally, being granted permits, the Kazet Theatre departs on its long-awaited tour of Europe. The performers' passports are their theatre-membership cards, which bear an image of a harp flanked by the twin-masks of tragedy and comedy poised above camp barracks ringed by barbed-wire fences.

They head south on a British military train. The sun lights up the landscape of their recent suffering. Many dwellings remain in ruins. Labourers are at work, clearing rubble, rebuilding. The theatre orchestra is playing and the performers are singing. It is summer, and they are in the first flush of freedom, light headed with excitement, like children on an excursion.

In Hanover, the ensemble is given a carriage of its own. A second carriage is set aside for props, sets and costumes. The train heads west towards the Dutch border. A cursory inspection of their permits, and the performers are allowed through with an ease that leaves them elated. It is night. The carriage is a world unto itself, the performers are cocooned in their private compartments, cradled by the swaying motion.

For six years, trains had conveyed them to death, and slave labour, cattle wagons enveloped in the stench of shit and fear, urine and vomit. Children clinging to mothers and fathers. Lover to lover. Friend to stranger. Fists pounding the walls, hands clawing the boards in panic; but on this train journey, at least, the memory is set aside; and in the morning, the sun is rising over a landscape alive with farmhouses and village paths of sunlit silver, church steeples and fields of crops nearing harvest. The countryside unfurls beneath open skies towards the horizon. Their daring venture has succeeded in ways the performers could never have believed possible.

Mid-afternoon, the train is on the outskirts of Brussels. The residents are going about their business. The streets are pervaded by a reassuring air of normality, and at the Brussels station there are delegations waiting to welcome them: Jewish community leaders, Belgian politicians, and former fighters in the Belgian underground. Colonel Lavreau, president of the Federation of Belgian Resistance Fighters and Prisoners of War in Germany, and Robert Vercauteren, president of the Association of Former Belgian Inmates of Bergen-Belsen. Monsieur Robert, members of the ensemble will call him.

Monsieur Robert walks with a limp from an injury he sustained as one of four hundred Belgian citizens incarcerated in Bergen-Belsen. Suddenly he stops. His eyes are wide open, as if arrested by an apparition. Sonia, too, has stopped in her tracks. Monsieur Robert and Sonia stare at each other.

Then Robert bursts out: 'Madame, give me back my tin cup.' The couple embrace and kiss, paying no heed to the circle of onlookers that has formed around them. They cannot believe they have found each other. Their reunion offers a rare glimpse of Sonia in the Bergen-Belsen concentration camp.

In the final weeks before liberation the typhus epidemic was at its height. The sick and the dying lay on their bunks. Others wandered the camp insane with hunger. They spent their nights dreaming of food and their days in anticipation of their meagre ration of bread. They queued for the slop that passed as turnip soup and the dirty liquid that was coffee.

The most treasured possession in the camp was a tin cup or a plate, any container. Without one, there was no food. Sonia's container was missing, perhaps lost, most likely stolen. A friend allowed her to use her cup when she was done, but by the time Sonia reached the table where the soup was distributed, the pot was often empty.

On this day, she does not have the strength to borrow the cup in time for her portion. She is consumed by hunger, and weeping. A group of male prisoners is marching by under the eye of an SS officer. One of the prisoners steps out from the ranks and runs to Sonia. 'Madame, why are you crying?' he asks. Too weak to talk, Sonia indicates with her hand that she has lost her cup.

Without hesitation, the prisoner unties his cup from the piece of cloth that holds up his trousers, and throws it to her. The SS officer is on him, beating him across the neck and back with his truncheon. 'Get back into line, you stinking dog,' he screams. The prisoners march on.

For weeks, the stranger's generous act and his beating are on Sonia's conscience. She wants to return the cup and thank him. She fears for his safety. She scours the camp in search of him and waits in the same spot day after day for a sight of the marching men. She will not see him again until their encounter at the Brussels station.

Monsieur Robert attends each rehearsal and performance. He showers the performers with gifts, shows them how to get around Brussels and pays for their tram tickets. He takes them on sight-seeing walks and sits with them in cafes where he speaks of his hatred of those who collaborated and his raging desire to bring them to justice.

He appoints the performers honorary members of the Association of Belgium Prisoners of Bergen-Belsen at a gala ceremony, and addresses them as fellow resistors returned from battle. Colonel Lavreau is also attentive. He visits them in the hotel at any hour, and asks them if there is anything he can do, if there is anything lacking.

On 16 June, the troupe premieres at the Patria Theatre. The performance is sold out. The boxes are filled with VIPs and parliamentarians. The audience is taken by the artistry, the expressionist sets, the haunting songs and the choreography, and the fierce energy and zeal that emanates from the performers in their unflinching portrayal of their suffering.

The ensemble members are invited to banquets, feted in private homes, cafes and restaurants, and praised at celebrations. Hotel guests and people in the streets recognise them from news items and extend their welcome. Parliamentarians and the minister of justice speak of their resolve and spirit. A motion is moved that the entire ensemble be granted residents' permits and fast-tracked to citizenship. The motion is greeted with standing applause and carried unanimously. The contrast with what the performers have known for most of their young lives is startling.

Newspaper reports sing the ensemble's praises. They are the troubadours of Auschwitz and Belsen, sprung from the underworld; young men and women, but old in what they have endured and witnessed. They are of a lineage that reaches back to the rivers of Babylon, and the embodiment of many exiles. They are history personified, and they are the future. Critics proclaim a new era in Yiddish theatre.

Sonia Boszkowska is singled out as a performer who would grace the stage of any theatre; and Sami Feder is the acclaimed director and the go-to man for interviews. He recounts the tale of his journey through his portals of hell, and of the Kazet Theatre's ascent from its daring beginnings to its triumph just months after liberation. He is overwhelmed by the warmth of the reception.

The performers crave that warmth, he says, but they are not here only to perform. They are duty bound to speak for those they have left behind in Bergen-Belsen and in camps throughout

Germany, Austria and Italy. Two years after liberation, a quarter of a million displaced persons are still waiting. Unable to return to their ruined homes, and not yet allowed to move on, they are in purgatory, the doors to many lands locked to them.

'We are here to show the world that we are not helpless victims,' says Sami. 'We are not the leftover waste of the ghettos, and we are not beggars. We do not want to be pitied. We are human beings. We have a right to freedom.' The theatre's political intent, Sami affirms, is to highlight the plight of their stateless brothers and sisters.

The ensemble performs five times in Brussels to sell-out houses and standing ovations. It presents evenings of cabaret and the plays *Two-hundred-thousand* and *The Enchanted Tailor*. They stage *The Redeemer,* and they sing the partisan anthem at the end of each performance.

Local companies have lent them props, costumes and professional lighting. The troupe is well-rehearsed and reaching new heights in its performance. Flowers and cards await the performers in their dressing rooms. Admirers applaud them as they leave the theatre. At receptions, they wear suits and elegant dresses. They appear calm and dignified and, for the first time in years, unburdened.

Monsieur Robert is at the Brussels station to farewell them. He embraces each member. We are comrades, he says, in the ongoing struggle against fascism.

The train heads north to the port city of Antwerp, where again the troupe performs to enthusiastic audiences. Members of the ensemble stroll in the evenings by the river estuary. They take in the smell of brine and sea breezes. They are invited into private homes and are welcomed as guests aboard an ocean liner.

The land has been unlocked, and they have reached the edge of the continent. The sea is a mystery evoking infinite possibilities. They stand on the deck and inhale the heady scent of distant voyages; and they leave Antwerp elated. After twenty-one days in Belgium they are buoyed by the momentum. They are heading to Paris, London, New York and Palestine.

They arrive in Paris on 3 July and are greeted by a guard of honour and a military band playing the Marseillaise. Only later do they learn that the band was not playing for them, but for a Belgian minister who had travelled on the same train.

The troupe is driven at night from the station to a hotel by members of the Jewish community and relief agencies. Prostitutes cruise the corridors and foyer. The air is fetid and the rooms are strewn with rubbish. The troupe is shunted through the backstreets of Paris till dawn in search of better accommodation.

The early days are endless rounds of bureaucratic formalities, questions over documents and permits and, again, an infernal waiting. Paris, as they had dreamt it, is a city of lights and ageing beauty, graced by legendary landmarks: the Arc de Triomphe, the Louvre and the Eiffel Tower, the Hotel de Ville and the Trocadero. But the streets are shabby, and the people harried and preoccupied. The city is gripped by political struggles, mass strikes, housing shortages and an epidemic of tuberculosis.

Refugees are crowded in cheap hotels and apartment buildings. In the third year after liberation, bread and coffee, cooking oil and sugar are still rationed. Bombed-out factories remain in ruins. On Bastille Day, the day after the theatre's arrival, there are military parades, fireworks, dancing in the streets and a night of celebration; but the next day the gloom returns.

The Belgian dream is fast receding. The members of the ensemble are being stripped of illusions and drained of energy. Their spirits plummet. In interviews, Sami Feder speaks of his disenchantment. We need your support, he says, as do our brothers and sisters stranded in the displaced camps in Germany and elsewhere. We cannot turn our back on them. They are marooned on the sites of their persecution. With each passing day, their morale is falling, yet the world remains silent. There is desperation in Sami's pleas. The ground is shifting beneath him.

In the last two weeks of July, the troupe performs in the Sarah Bernhardt theatre. They are finally welcomed at a community banquet. Sami Feder is hailed as the father of the troupe, and Sonia as its leading actor and co-founder. The performers are lauded for their skills and hailed as a symbol of rebirth and survival. Their fortunes appear to be changing, but within days their hopes are crushed.

France is struggling to cope with a surge of displaced persons and orphaned children. Relief agencies are overwhelmed by the concerns of Parisians returning to their expropriated businesses and properties. There is not enough money to go around. The ensemble members are just thirty among many thousands.

In Paris, the members of the troupe must fend for themselves. They are short of funds, hungry and exhausted, and reliant on welfare. They are refugees all over again, a wandering troupe in search of an audience in a vast metropolis. Sami is frantic in his efforts to save the theatre. He conducts interviews with the editors of Yiddish journals, and points to letters of invitation from overseas sponsors.

But the performers' backers are deserting them. The relief workers are overworked and indifferent. Theatre and the arts are low on their list of priorities. Impresarios in the US are in search of light entertainment, wary of the confronting tales enacted by the ensemble. They are not prepared to finance a troupe of thirty on a national tour: the costs of wages, accommodation, theatre hire and travel expenses are too high.

Tours to London, New York and Buenos Aires are cancelled. Sami has no choice but to disband the troupe and allow its members to go their own ways. It could not last. In their gathering lay their future dissolution, in their unity lay the seeds of their dispersal, and in their performances they had paved a way from the past to the future. It was time to move on.

Some stay on in Paris in the homes of friends and relatives. Others receive visas from sponsors in the Americas, or seek passage to Palestine. Some have no option but to return to Bergen-Belsen. Among them are Sami and Sonia. Again, a train journey, backtracking over borders they had so recently crossed. Again, rails leading to guarded portals. Returned, as they had left, to the republic of the stateless.

Sami and Sonia eventually return to Paris. They marry in 1950. Time hangs in the balance. The authority that Sami had forged in Frankfurt and Berlin appears to be slipping; his focus is shifting. As the need to document what he has witnessed takes hold of him, Sonia wants to move on. She wants to step out into the world. She wants to live and make a living. She is looking forward. Sami is condemned to look back.

Responding to a small item in a Yiddish journal, on 27 August 1951, Sami writes:

> Somewhere in a small corner, on page three, hidden behind a barrage of news, there is a report: 'The last displaced persons camp in Germany, the British Zone, has been liquidated.' A chapter of history closed. Shush. Silence. As if nothing had happened. Bergen-Belsen where thousands of martyrs were buried in the weeks following liberation, forgotten. Bergen-Belsen is not even named, and the dead are not mentioned. The displaced persons camps in the British zone have been closed, and not a tear shed for the memory of those who are buried there—souls who could never come with us.
>
> How does the word 'liquidate' sound to those who survived and spent years of their lives there? Bergen-Belsen cannot be liquidated. It exists. Thirty thousand corpses lie there, and tens of thousands more lie in unmarked graves, murdered on the brink of liberation. For us Bergen-Belsen will exist forever. *Yiskor.* Always remembered.

After Sami settles in Israel in 1962 he will not return to live theatre. He will not direct or perform again. He will spend his remaining years retracing his journey, crisscrossing that span of time from 1925 till 1947 recounting the same stories in many versions. He will write: 'Forgive me, I am slow on the typewriter.

I do not have money for editors, and no resources for technical help. I do not have time to correct my work. Forgive me if I repeat myself.'

Yet no matter how much he writes, he will say there is much more to write, and that he is too ill and tired, and time is running out, and that even with his best will and strenuous efforts, he can never depict all he had seen and experienced. 'But I will try,' he says. 'I will draw on every ounce of strength I have left to fulfil my sacred mission.'

He will live in the promised land, but Bergen-Belsen will remain his Jerusalem. He will forever sing the praises of the Kazet Theatre and the republic of the stateless. He will name its triumphs: the kindergartens, schools, trade workshops, folk university, the houses of learning and yeshivas, its own court and police force, library and adult education courses, the music school, dance school, newspapers and journals. The miracle.

And he will sit by the water of the Mediterranean and vow: 'If I forget thee, O Bergen-Belsen, let my right hand forget its skill. Let my tongue cleave to the roof of my mouth, if I remember thee not; if I set Bergen-Belsen above my highest joy.'

I now suspect that Sami's highest joy was his love for Sonia, but it is a joy he did not record. He documents Sonia's seminal role in the Kazet Theatre; but he does not hint at what he felt for her.

I look for clues elsewhere. I recall the first time I saw Sonia perform, circa 1980, as a guest overseas artist, on the Kadimah stage, in Elsternwick, a seven-minute drive from the city's beaches, and an easy walk from the Joyce Street house that years later she would share with Pinche; and a ten-minute drive from the aged-care home where she would spend her final decade.

The stage is modest, a raised platform. There are no curtains; the back wall is wood panelled and flanked by vertical stained-glass windows. The hall seats upwards of two hundred. On the walls are black-and-white photos of writers and actors and community leaders posing with dignified expressions. Sonia stands at the mic. Her hair is dyed blonde. She wears a pale blue dress that hugs her slim figure.

There are survivors in the audience. They do not see themselves as victims, and they do not live as victims. They have moved on with their lives and are happy to see each other. They are here to be entertained and to hear songs they have known since childhood. Sonia is at one with them. She performs pre-war songs of hope and promise: 'We are young, the world is open'. Yiddish cabaret: 'Why do you loiter outside my window?'

She switches to French and Russian: Edith Piaf and 'Play Balalaika'. She sings nonsense songs: 'Listen to this story children, listen with nose and eye, over grandma babushka's roof, a cow I saw did fly'. And songs of nostalgia: 'Where is that village, where is that street? Where is that laneway where we would meet?'

She does not perform ghetto songs in concert. They are reserved for memorial evenings. There is one exception: *Springtime*, written in the Vilna ghetto by her friend, Shmerke Kaczerginski, songwriter, poet, frontline artist and, like Sami, by trade a printer.

Shmerke was born in Vilna, Lithuania, in 1908; he was a year younger than Sami. His mother and father died when he was six and, like Sami, he was raised by his grandfather. Shmerke was a leading light in the movement of experimental Yiddish poets in Vilna known as the 'Young Ones'. When the Germans occupied Vilna in June 1941, he posed as a deaf mute to evade capture. He was caught in early 1942 and incarcerated in the Vilna Ghetto.

Now Shmerke wrote songs reflecting his people's struggles: ballads of partisans and ghetto fighters, songs of mourning and bleak lullabies, 'Quiet, quiet, let's be silent, corpses are growing here'. His works were performed in ghetto cabarets, theatre evenings and cultural gatherings.

After the Vilna Ghetto uprising in September 1943, Shmerke escaped to the forests and served as a partisan in the borderlands of Lithuania and Byelorussia. He re-entered Vilna with the Soviet Army on 13 July 1944, on the day of the city's liberation. After the war Shmerke lived for a time in Lodz, then settled in Paris in 1946 and toured displaced persons camps in Germany, where he met Sonia and Sami.

Like Sami, Shmerke became a collector of songs and folklore, an archivist and a historian. In 1948, he published his crowning achievement, the landmark 435-page *Songs of the Ghettos and Concentration Camps.* Shmerke moved to Buenos Aires in 1950 and embarked on speaking tours and concerts in Europe and throughout North and South America.

He died in 1954 in a plane crash in the Andes foothills. He was returning home from a public engagement in the provincial town of Mendoza.

Shmerke wrote *Springtime* in the Vilna Ghetto, after the death of his first wife, Barbara Kaufman. Barbara was captured and taken prisoner in Krakow for her role in the Resistance. She was deported to the Vilna Ghetto where she met Shmerke. The couple were married in 1942 and were active in the ghetto underground. Barbara was executed in 1943. It was springtime:

> I wander the ghetto, from alley to alley, but nowhere can I find peace. Where is my lover? How can I recover? People, say something, a word to console me. My house is lit up now, by skies blue and glowing. But what good does it do me? I stand like a beggar, by each doorway, and beg for the sunlight.
>
> I go to my workplace, and pass by our cottage, in sorrow the door is locked tight. The day fierce with sunrays, the flowers are wilting. They weep, for them it is night. Each evening, returning, my sadness is burning. Right here you'd be waiting. Right here in the shadows, your footsteps familiar, you embraced and kissed me.
>
> This year, the springtime has arrived early. My longing for you in full bloom. I see you approaching, laden with flowers. With joy, you are coming to me. The sun has watered the garden with sunrays. The earth is coated in green. My dear one, my lover. Where have you vanished? I can't get you out of my mind.
>
> Springtime, please take my sorrow, and return my lover, my dear one to me. Springtime, upon your wings of blue, take my heart with you, and return my joy to me.

Sonia stands on the Kadimah stage and sways to *Springtime*'s tango rhythm. I knew little about her then. I did not know that hers was the final voice heard by some of the inmates she sang to in Bergen-Belsen in the months before liberation. Sonia in rags, surrounded by death and terror, singing.

I can never know what songs she sang back then. Perhaps a song of resistance, a children's song. A lullaby: *Sleep my child, my life, my treasure. Ai-le-lu-le-lu. Sleep my child, my prayer, my future. Ai-le-lu-le-lu. Fortunate is she who has a mother. And a cradle too. Ai-le-lu-le-lu.*

It is in song that I find Sonia. A song is finite, a framed moment of intensity. It has time limits, set boundaries. In song, Sonia felt at home and protected. And it is in *Springtime* and her performance of it, that I picture them, Sonia and Sami, in the time of their highest joy and their deepest sadness.

The song returns me to Sami, on a winter night—10 February 1945. Bunzlau slave labour camp. The inmates cannot sleep. They hear the pounding of heavy artillery. The following morning, they are not ordered out for work. Instead, they are assembled and told that the camp is to be closed, and the able-bodied transferred to another labour camp. The sick and the weak will follow later.

Late into the night, the men pace the barracks, calculating. Some are on their feet, praying. Some sit by the table, engaged in whispered conversation. Others lie on their bunks, fully dressed, awaiting the next move, dozing. The Soviet front is closing in from the east, and the Allied armies are approaching from the west.

There are rumours that the SS are planning to raze the camp and poison the sick prisoners. The debate rages: should the sick inmates try to disguise their ailments? Should the able-bodied feign illness, and stay put in the hope of being liberated by the Russians, or should they leave with their overseers?

At 1.30 am, there's an uneasy stillness. Suddenly the screams of SS guards: '*Achtung! Achtung!* All able-bodied men out to the assembly ground. Ready to march. *Schnell.* You have ten minutes. Do you understand?' '*Jawohl,*' the men reply from the barracks, in one thunderous chorus.

They hastily dress, gather their meagre belongings and rush from the barracks, hearts pounding. The snow crunches underfoot; the moon peeps in and out of black clouds. They line up, eight to a row, and stand to attention. Their overseers pace the lines, guns at the ready.

There is no headcount, no selection, and no search for those who have opted to remain hidden. The wagons have been loaded with ammunition and provisions. Some of the inmates are harnessed to the wagons. The camp commandant orders the march to begin. The convoy of slaves and their masters files out in the darkness. Some of the wagons are bogged in the snow. The guards beat the men, screaming: 'You useless pigs. Do you want to pull, or do you want to die?' The men are soaked in sweat. Palls of frost rise with their breath.

The convoy moves on. Blows rain down on the men when their pace slackens. Many collapse, exhausted. Some beg permission to load their fallen comrades onto wagons. Others heave them onto their shoulders, and haul them over the snow, willing their feet on beyond the limits of endurance.

At night, the men sleep in barns, in camp barracks and in the fields, cuddling in the snow for warmth. The days become weeks and still the march continues: past burning homes, bombed-out villages and gutted factories littered with debris and metal. Searchlights sweep the landscape. The air trembles with the roar of planes, and the earth shudders with the thud of bombs and anti-aircraft fire.

Sami Feder will record the details of the march in his memoirs: the fate of his comrades, their names and the manner of their deaths recorded. He will write of the beatings, and of marchers murdered on a whim by guards enraged by the advance of the liberating armies. And of the SS men, machine guns in hand, marching at the rear of the column, shooting those who fell behind, and leaving them for dead by the wayside.

He will write of crossing a river and of the bridge exploding moments later. The men are flung off their feet, and they fall covered in dirt, blood and mortar. He will write of prisoners breaking free and making a run for it, then betrayed and smoked out of their hideouts and executed by SS men and civilian militias; and of being ordered to bury dead comrades, and reciting the *Kaddish,* the prayer for the dead, over their corpses.

He will write of men being lined up to be shot, then reprieved by the counter-orders of a 'decent' commander; of nights sleeping in abandoned camp huts, and of the floorboards being set alight to flush out prisoners who had secreted themselves beneath them. And of life reduced to footsteps on snow, the crunch of one foot and then the other, each step edging closer to death or—dare the prisoners hope—freedom.

After six weeks on the march, the convoy arrives at the

Mittelbrau-Dora slave labour complex. The dwindling band of sick and exhausted men is marched to the sub-camp, Ellrich, which produces V-1 flying bombs and V-2 rockets. Of all the camps that Sami has endured in the past four years, Ellrich will prove to be the worst.

It is crowded with prisoners from many nations, housed in barracks and hangars. The men are marched to and from the quarries in round-the-clock shifts, seven days a week, each completing a work day of up to sixteen hours. When a prisoner falls ill, his forehead is marked by a number, and he is consigned to a barrack stacked with corpses squeezed between layers of timber, where he too will await cremation.

Sami will write of the anti-Semitic attacks by fellow inmates, and the brutal hierarchies among the prisoners. And of the saving graces: his *Kapo*, the barracks leader, a gypsy called Peter who, believing they share the same name, grants Feder favours; and a slave-labour mate from white Russia, who shares a mutual love of literature and theatre—their whispered conversations help them pass the long days loading clay and gravel onto wagons.

One morning, the prisoners make their way to the assembly ground for the daily headcount and trek to work. They are told that the camp is to be evacuated. The front is closing in; the sound of machine gun and artillery is growing louder. The men are marched from the camp, loaded into cattle wagons and taken north, to the city of Hamburg.

The British have bombed the tracks. The train is left stranded at the Hamburg station. After his liberation, Sami learns that the prisoners were to be shipped onto the Elbe River, and drowned.

Instead, they are transported to Bergen-Belsen. They arrive in the last days of March.

After years on the move, yet another camp is his destination; again, the sight of barbed wire, sentry huts and watchtowers, and beyond the wire, wooden huts and the ghostly movement of grey masses. Camp 1, the main camp, is overcrowded with the sick and the dying. The newcomers are incarcerated in Camp 2, in the military barracks of the Panzer Training School, sections of which, in the months before liberation, housed prisoners of war: Sami's final portal.

Sunday, 15 April 1945. Sami and his comrades lie in the barracks. They are too weak to move. The sun mocks them through the windows. They are dreaming of their daily bowl of soup. They crave water, but do not possess the energy to fetch it. Suddenly, the sound of gunfire. The barracks are shaking. The firing grows louder; the men cling to their bunks. A deafening roar, and the windows are shattered. The barracks are being strafed by low-flying German aeroplanes. Some of the men are dead, others lie wounded in pools of blood.

Then the thunder of cannon fire, and soon after, the rumbling of jeeps and tanks. Several prisoners shuffle to the window. 'Comrades,' one of them shouts. 'The English!' The men cannot believe it. Minutes later, a voice can be heard through a loud-hailer. 'Prisoners of all nations...the British military has taken the camp. You are free.'

The inmates are free, but not free. It is a line that Sami will repeat many times in his memoirs. They are free, but the dead lie side-by-side with the sick and the dying. The spirit is momentarily lighter, but the body is not. Ah, sweet liberation, yet for many a new battle is about to begin. They are free of the spectre of death, but do not know what it means to walk among the living.

And there are dangers: the inmates of the Horror Camp are quarantined for fear of the spread of typhus. During the first two days, Hungarian SS guards—who have been retained by the conditions of a truce to help maintain order—patrol the barracks. Some of them shoot newly liberated inmates for attempting to leave the camp in search of food or for raiding a potato patch, or 'stealing' supplies from the camp food stores: a final pretext for murder.

The first Sabbath after liberation, several hundred survivors gather in the camp grounds. Many are still weak and exhausted. They huddle together for warmth. A voice rises from the stillness humming a *nigun,* a melody. From the humming there arises a song, and from the song, a collective singing.

The first stars appear. A bonfire is lit. Sami Feder stands by the fire and recites his newly written poems of *umkum un oifkum,* death and resurrection. Rabbi Zwi Helfgott, a former Yugoslav prisoner of war, presides over the gathering. He raises his fists and proclaims: 'Death to the fascists. Long live freedom.'

He lifts a burning log from the fire and recites *Havdalah,* the prayer marking the end of the Sabbath, and leads the survivors in song. They rock back and forth as they sing. Some struggle to their feet, and dance by the fire. It is a scene that will remain forever engraved in Sami's soul.

~

Over the ensuing weeks, the inmates of Camp 1 are moved to Camp 2 and housed in the former living quarters of German officers. Bergen-Belsen, now a displaced persons camp, is a vast sanatorium. Some of the able-bodied men are taken on military trucks to a displaced persons camp in the town of Celle, twenty kilometres away, among them Sami. Within weeks, he decides to return to Bergen-Belsen. In his mind, his project to retrieve the works written and sung in the camps and ghettos is forming.

I imagine Sami's return. The winter is long over. There are scenes of serenity: forests of birch and conifers, creeks fringed with willows. Groves of linden and ash. Heathland and juniper. Village streets lined with picket fences and timber cottages. Here and there, a shattered house, blown up culverts and bridges—warped steel and shattered concrete partly submerged in water. The roads are crawling with military convoys, cut off by checkpoints.

The truck approaches Bergen-Belsen. Uniformed soldiers guard the gate. Sami feels a tightening in the chest, a moment of panic, but the guards appear benign and his papers are in order. There are no demands barked by enraged officers, and no killer dogs straining on their leashes. He is waved through.

The camp grounds are vast. There are jeeps driven by military personnel and motor vehicles idling. Uniformed nurses climb the steps to the camp hospital. A truck filled with sacks of potatoes is being unloaded. Women peg washing to cords strung between makeshift poles made from stripped branches. Men and women walk the pathways, some shuffling like phantoms.

Sami sees her from a distance. She is thin. He is not sure at first. It is four years since he last saw her. Perhaps he is dreaming. He catches the glint of sun on the red-tiled roof. As she draws closer, Sami grows more certain. Then she lights up in recognition. She stops. She sways on her feet, closes her eyes, clenches her fists, and presses her knuckles to her eyelids.

Sami does not dare move closer. The sounds around him have faded to silence. She opens her eyes, and they are clear; her face is transparent. She quickens her steps. Sami is thirty-nine, Sonia twenty-five, but time has lost meaning; all is reduced to this moment, two people embracing.

Sami and Sonia's fists are unclenched, and their hands are open. Beneath the palms, the rise and fall of breath, the heartbeat of the living. The armour that has sustained them is falling away. There is no frontline, no need for resistance. There is only Sami and Sonia. Love lost. Love regained. Springtime in the republic of the stateless.

Maybe this is how it was. Maybe. But of his return from Celle to Bergen-Belsen and this meeting with Sonia, Sami writes only in passing. 'There I met my *khaverte*, my comrade, Sonia Boszkowska, who had performed theatre under my direction in the Benzin Muse ensemble in Poland. We decided to create a theatre studio.' And, later, another reference: 'Immediately after the liberation, as hundreds were expiring every day from typhus, exhaustion and hunger, it was then, among the dying, that I met my *khaverte*, Sonia Boszkowska.' That is all.

~

There are images captured by British war photographers and eyewitness accounts by the British troops. 'We had seen the dead and the wounded on battlefields, but we had never seen anything like this.' 'The things I saw completely defy description.' 'It was so different to, well to anything.' 'I can't explain it... We'd seen distressed people about, people walking from town to town, but nothing like this.' 'No words can describe the horror of this place.' The phrase most used: 'There are no words for this.'

And there are the sounds most remembered—an eerie stillness, the impression of a city of the dead peopled by phantoms. Many of those who remain alive wandered about, staring at their liberators with incredulous eyes, as if to say, are we dreaming? There is apathy and rage and a thirst for summary justice. Crowds of inmates assemble each day by the pits to scream at their former tormentors as they transport the corpses for mass burial. Sonia is somewhere in all of this.

The sun shone in those days, but the light it shed was dulled by an oppressive haze, hanging over tracts of barren heathland littered with bodies. And up close, in the huts, the feverish inmates: heads shaven; skin ravaged by bedsores, scabies and ulcers; bodies reduced to stick-like limbs, exposed ribs, jutting chins and shrunken faces.

That first embrace between Sonia and Sami—if there was one—would have been between two near skeletons. Sonia may have been too weak to stand up, too exhausted to embrace. She had barely made it to the day of her liberation, and Sami had barely made it to the final camp. They had survived. That is all.

There was a cleansing station that came to be called the 'human laundry'. The inmates were stripped of their rags, wrapped in blankets, stretchered from the huts in Camp 1 to an ambulance and driven to the station, which was housed in a converted stable in Camp 2. They were attended by German nurses now acting under British military orders.

At first, the nurses were hostile, but when the emaciated inmates were stretchered in, they were horrified by what they saw, and they worked, week after week from eight in the morning till six at night, until they were sick and exhausted. Several died after contracting typhus.

There were two rows of ten stalls either side of a passageway. Each one with a table, a bucket of water, towels and soap and scrubbing brushes. A mobile bath unit supplied hot water. The inmates were scrubbed and shaved, and dusted with DDT as disinfectant. Then they were dressed in fresh clothes, wrapped in clean blankets and transferred to improvised hospital wards in converted compounds or to outdoor beds and straw pallets. Fourteen thousand inmates underwent this process. Sonia could well have been one of them.

There is one memory that he did share with me of her final weeks in Bergen-Belsen before liberation. She is lying ill with typhus. She is close to death. Her will is ebbing. A fellow inmate is tugging at her arms. Imploring. 'Sonia. Stand up.' She is dragging Sonia to her feet. 'If you want to live, you must stand up.'

~

Sami too was ill. He was designated 'fit' by the relativities of triage; but this meant only that he could stand up unaided. He wrote in his memoirs that, one month after liberation, his flesh and bones remained eaten by hunger. His lungs were scarred, and he would spend time in a TB sanatorium and undergo surgeries in Paris and Berlin. He struggled with insomnia, heart problems and periods of depression. The doctors warned him to avoid the physical and mental demands of theatre.

Sami revisits one incident in several memoirs. It takes place in the early months of 1946. The Kazet Theatre is well established, and the premier performance is long over. Sami is preoccupied with the many demands of the theatre and camp politics. He is walking in the camp grounds. A military truck veers onto the pavement. The driver, a British soldier, had been drinking.

Sami is catapulted head first to the pavement. He is rushed to the camp hospital with his skull fractured in two places. He undergoes a life-saving operation and spends six weeks in hospital recuperating. Sonia sits at his bedside. She reads to him, transcribes scripts and helps him plan future performances. Perhaps this extended period of convalescence brought Sami and Sonia closer. But the injuries Sami sustained also had a more lasting impact: he would suffer migraines for the rest of his life.

Sonia spoke to me only once of the death marches. She recounted a tale of a dream: The women have halted for the night. It is snowing. They lie in squalor, freezing and exhausted. Sonia drifts into an uneasy sleep. She is falling, then she is rising from the earth. She is taking flight. Her comrades, in their misery, are fading far below her. She soars over field and forest, towns and cities. She is at ease and buoyant. The air is light and the skies are transparent. If only, she thinks—if only I could keep flying forever.

Sonia would not speak of the horrors. But within months of liberation she was re-enacting them—and this is what her audiences, the 'surviving remnants', wanted. It was a plea British soldiers reported hearing in their early encounters with the inmates: 'Tell the world! Tell the world! Did you know what was happening? Tell the world! They must know what happened to us!'

Yes, there are tales that are meant to be told, and not to tell them would be a betrayal. Sami and Sonia, I hope I have done your tales justice. That I have not betrayed you. The thought is unbearable.

Where We Meet

Been not enough listening. Not enough sitting. Sitting on the earth, sitting on the veranda. Sitting in the shade beneath the house. The land, as far as the eye can see, clad in ochres and reds. The sky so blue it hurts. The air so dry it sucks in the breath. Yet it is cool enough in the shade to converse, and there's time enough to take in the silence, to notice that far-distant cloud. 'It's going to rain,' the old man says. 'Give it six hours, but believe me it's going to rain. Best place to be is here, sitting in the shade beneath the house.'

This is a tale of maps: some of country where the people have lived for sixty thousand years. Perhaps many more. Could be the Kimberley, the red centre, or somewhere up north. Could be a remote settlement, a parched riverbed, or the dusty streets of an outback town. The place will remain unnamed. I am a guest. Learning to see what I have never seen, hearing stories I have never heard. I am here to listen, and to exchange tales. In search of that place where we meet.

The kitchen is where my parents sat late at night. Hadassah and Meier. In a single-fronted terrace, built against the light, enclosed in stucco and brick. Cool enough to preserve ugly patches of damp. When they moved in, the roof slates were slipping, the walls were cracked and the rooms infested with rats. There was a housing shortage back then and the landlord could do what he liked.

My parents got rid of the rats, repaired the roof, plastered the cracks and got on with their lives. And late at night they sat in the kitchen with their old-world friends. I strained to hear them as I lay in bed. Their voices, as in a lullaby, sang the names of places on a distant map. *Bransk, Bialystok, Grodek, Orly, Bielsk.* Border country, where the armies of rival kingdoms were forever on the march.

It ended badly. The lucky ones got out. Some sailed for a new world and settled in Melbourne, a city at the ends of the earth. Yet, no matter how far they'd sailed, they could not escape the longing for the place of their birth and the horror at what had happened to those they left behind. I lived in a house of absences and ghosts, and one photo album of my parents' pre-war past.

'Who are these people?' I asked of one photo.

'Three of my six sisters, one of my three brothers, your uncle Joshua, your grandmother, Khane-Esther. Your cousins Khaimke and Freda, eleven and six years old.'

'Where are they, now?'

'I don't want to talk about it,' Hadassah would say. And that was that. Of nine siblings, her parents and extended family, only three survived. On my father's side, it appeared, there was no one left.

In 1986, I made the journey, travelling alone, rucksack on my back, on the Trans-Siberian from Beijing across the length of the Soviet empire to Moscow and beyond. I entered the Polish borderlands by train from the east; walked the streets of towns, villages and cities whose names I had heard as I drifted asleep on the other side of the world: *Bransk, Bialystok, Grodek, Orly, Bielsk.* Places that they now called the old world, *der alter velt.*

When I returned, I sat with Hadassah in the kitchen of that single-fronted house. I now had the means to invoke the ghosts. 'Saw birch trees the length of the empire,' I tell her, 'ghostly white. Standing alone, standing in packs.'

'The *beryosé,*' she says, as if in a trance, and she sings, in Yiddish, the mother tongue: *O come quiet evening, and rock the fields to sleep/ We sing you a song of praise, oh quiet evening glow/ How still it has become, the night has come to stay/ The white beryosé, remains standing in the forest alone.* Mother tells stories through song. It is too painful to tell them in prose.

With Meier, I sit on a bench in Curtain Square, the neighbourhood park, beneath an archway of Moreton Bay figs, six abreast on either side of a gravel path. Here is where we meet in the months after my return. The square is home territory; the kindergarten I attended is across the road, and the primary school a two-minute walk. The square is where we drift, father and son, between our words. The silences are broken by a gust of breeze, the bark of a dog, and tales sparked by the names of distant streets I have now walked.

'Sienkievitza Avenue,' I say.

'Ah, that's where Kondruchik the White Russian sold ice-cream, and where we played billiards and chess, and where, in the Macedonian quarter, we ate Turkish delight, and where horse-drawn carriages dashed by on their way to the dance halls on

Saturday nights.' Meier's stories flow quickly now that I know the maps.

There is another map: an item I first saw in a museum exhibition in Melbourne in 1994. I knew instantly where I had seen such a map before. Eight years earlier, on that journey to Poland, in a pavilion in a forest of birch and pine—on the outskirts of the site where Treblinka death camp once stood. That map detailed places of massacre in an area that extended east to the Soviet border and beyond, and hundreds of kilometres to the west.

On the Treblinka site is an assembly of stones, seventeen thousand in all. Each one is said to represent a town, city or hamlet from which the eight hundred thousand men, women and children who died here were transported one generation ago.

I searched among the stones for the names I'd first heard from the kitchen while I lay in bed as a child. *Bransk, Grodek, Orly, Bielsk.* I could not find them. I lit a candle in front of the stone marked *Bialystok,* the eastern Polish city where my father was born and where my mother's family moved when she was a child—the city where Hadassah and Meier lived the first three decades of their lives, and which they left. Just in time.

Now I am standing in front of that museum exhibit: a map of Victoria, my home state. Titled the *Massacre Map,* it shows sixty-eight sites of known killings of Indigenous people between 1836 and 1853. A caption adds: 'Many thousands more died beyond prying eyes.'

And I am contemplating a mystery: Why have I never heard of these sites? And why is it that in all my years living in the city where my family settled a year after I was born had I not once heard of the words Wurundjeri, Woiwurrung, Kulin?

I played on the banks of the Yarra River as a boy, sifted for yabbies with nets, launched myself on ropes into its muddy waters and swam in its brown depths. Why did I not know the ancient name: Birrarung, river of mists? Why did I not know of the clans who fished it, swam it and gathered on its banks? And why was it that after so many journeys to the beaches of the bay, I did not know of the Boonwurrung, the people of the coast? Why did I not know of the ancient maps?

'Where can I find out more?' I ask the exhibition curator, Jim Berg. Gundidjmara man. 'Go see Aunty Joy,' he says.

Weeks later I drive sixty kilometres northeast. I pull up in Healesville, in the driveway of a weatherboard house. There's a grandeur here at the feet of the mountains of the Great Divide, a clarity that comes after days of rain. Clouds drift from the upper slopes. Magpies and kookaburras hover by the veranda in anticipation of their daily feed.

Wurundjeri elder Joy Murphy Wandin opens the door and invites me into a house that contains millennia of history. She puts the kettle on the stove. On the living-room wall is a black-and-white photo taken in the early years of the twentieth century. Like the photo of my mother's family, there are nine people in two rows.

In the centre, at the back, stands Joy's grandfather, Robert Wandin—also known as Wandoon. White-haired, wearing a waistcoat and suit, he stands beside his wife, Jemima. She is dressed in a high-necked white blouse and a dark ankle-length skirt. Robert and Jemima are surrounded by six of their ten children and a family friend. The youngest child, an infant, is Joy's father, James Wandin. The photo radiates dignity and pride.

Robert was the nephew of William Barak, *Ngurungaeta*, the leader of a Wurundjeri clan, says Aunty Joy. That is the term to use, she says. *Ngurungaeta.* It is a word unto itself. No translation can do it justice, she says. Aunty Joy offers her knowledge like a gift.

In June 1835, as a young boy, William Barak, it is said, was present when John Batman signed the so-called treaty with elders of the Kulin. Treaty or no treaty, within decades the lands were taken, and the Woiwurrung language driven underground. The Indigenous population radically reduced through massacre and imported disease. The invasion was all but complete.

Aunty Joy knows her ancient maps well. In 1987, as a project officer for Aboriginal Affairs Victoria, Joy set out with anthropologist Alistair Brooks on a twenty-month journey to retrace the Aboriginal boundaries in the state. The pair consulted elders, and examined maps drawn by previous anthropologists, who had gathered the information from Indigenous peoples when their dispossession had just begun.

The Wurundjeri is a clan of the Woiwurrung language group, Aunty Joy tells me. The two names have in recent times become almost synonymous. Theirs is a territory ranging from the mountains of the Great Divide east to Mt Baw Baw, west to the Werribee River, and south towards the Boonwurrung lands by the coast. The Woiwurrung and the Boonwurrung are two of the five peoples who make up a confederation known as the Kulin.

As Aunty Joy speaks, the map takes shape. The foundations I have known since infancy are shifting beneath my feet. She is speaking of ancient times, yet for me she is charting new ground: the lands she speaks of had been hidden, the maps erased.

Yet the stories were passed on, knowledge exchanged, and fragments of language retained, in living rooms and at kitchen tables, on verandas and around fires, in distant exile or on Kulin land. There were always those who knew who they were and those who were hungry to know more; and always children who heard the ancestral names.

In the 1980s, the Wandin family commissioned anthropologist Diane Barwick to work with them to compile a family tree. Joy spreads the documents on the living room table, tracing the Wandin family five generations back.

There are names of renowned *Ngurungaeta*, says Joy: Ningulabul, the songman, whose people lived in the Macedon area; Billibellary and his son, Simon Wonga. Bebejan and his wife, Tooterie, a woman of knowledge, whose kin lived on the Yarra banks, in the area where the city now stands. And their son, Beruk, born in the Yarra Valley, circa 1824—William Barak for European ears.

As a child Barak saw the invaders arrive. He witnessed the theft of his peoples' lands and saw them corralled in mission stations and on reserves. He was present with his cousin Simon Wonga and other survivors from the Kulin clans, as they tried to secure land in 1859, at Acheron, a station north of the Great Divide. They were forced eight kilometres out, to the Mohican Run—'Cold Country' the Kulin called it—when a local grazier took possession of their fertile patch.

Barak was with them in 1862, back in Acheron, as they attempted again to work the land. They were joined by lay preachers, John Green and his wife Mary, recent immigrants from Scotland, who would become trusted allies and friends. Again, local graziers intervened. It fell to Barak and Wonga, accompanied by John Green, to lead their dispossessed peoples in search of a new haven in the territory that had, until so recently, been their secure home.

Today Acheron is a bus stop on the highway dissecting a valley of vineyards and fenced estates. Cattle country. Grazing herds lift their heads and gaze warily at passers-by. Many times, in the years since Aunty Joy opened her door, I have imagined the trek, a band of forty men, women and children, in March 1863, making their way from Acheron back south.

The route would have led past the razor-backed Cathedral Range. They would have encountered loggers and graziers, and teamsters on timber wagons with steel-rimmed wheels. They crossed the Divide by way of the Black Spur, on a track the Wurundjeri had cleared on previous treks.

I think of them whenever I travel the Black Spur Drive with its hairpin bends, flanked by forests of mountain ash and embankments thick with lichens and ferns. And I think of them on the descent—the hardest part of the trek behind them—into an expanse of fertile valley, in search of a new Eden on their ancient lands.

They finally settled, Aunty Joy tells me, on the banks of Badger Creek, near its confluence with the Birrarung, a

Wurundjeri camping site chosen by Wonga and Barak. They named it Coranderrk, after the mauve and cream flowering bush that grew there. Thinking, perhaps, at least here we will be safe.

We sit in the living room, Faris, Majida and I. The one-bedroom flat is on the second floor of a public housing estate, a twenty-minute walk from where I grew up, at the northern limits of my childhood beat. It is well kept and neat. The living-room floor is polished boards, and the kitchen floor is covered in linoleum, patterned in alternating squares of light and dark blue.

Whenever I visit there is food on the coffee table: bowls of almonds, cashews and pistachios, Majida's walnut and date scones and her home-baked cakes. Our shoes are shelved on the front door rack. From the sofa, where we sit, there is a view through the open doorway to the kitchen window and the upper branches of a tree. In winter the branches are bare; in spring they are thick with leaves. In autumn, they are cloaked in auburns and golds. Mid-afternoon the chatter of children on the way home from school can be heard. Inside, all is still.

'With Faris I am lucky,' Majida says. 'He looks like my dad. He says the things my dad said, and, like my dad, he is patient.' Turning to Faris, she says, 'I am lucky to be with you. We suffer the same fate.'

'I am like the wind,' says Faris, 'one hour good, the next hour bad. I feel hot all the time.'

No matter how often she has heard him say this, Majida follows every word. She is with him as his spirit rises, and with him when it falls.

'We suffer the same fate,' she repeats. 'Our great-grandfathers were Feyli Kurds who came to Iraq from Iran. We were both born in Iraq: Faris in Wasit, me in Baghdad. Faris in 1968, me in 1967. I lost my mother at thirteen, Faris lost his father at the same age. I looked after my younger brothers and sisters, and he looked after his.

'Our families were deported from Iraq back to Iran: Faris lived in Yazd, and I in Teheran. I sailed from Indonesia by boat in 2000, Faris in 2001. I settled in Sydney, Faris in Melbourne. And after all that time we met.

Turning to Faris she says, 'Faris, that is why I understand you. That is why when you are sleeping in the day time, I don't wake you.'

Faris cannot sleep. He paces the rooms late at night. He watches television into the early hours but cannot sit still. He walks to subdue his thoughts. He follows the beat of his feet. He walks the neighbouring streets, the gravel paths of Princes Park and, further afield, past the cafes in Sydney Road, seeking the comfort of city lights.

When he does sleep, it is in short bursts—from nine till noon, from noon till three, and from four until the fall of night. Even as he sleeps there is no respite. He dreams of the boat going under, and of his wife, Layla, and his daughter, Zahra. They are in the ocean. His daughter's hand is in his. She slips from his grasp. He follows her, but she is like melting butter, disappearing, reappearing. Vanishing.

Years later he sings to her as he sleeps. The same Arabic lullaby night after night. It is Majida who hears it. She is woken by his restless turning and his faltering voice. She watches him mouthing the words. She listens as his breath eases and he returns to sleep.

Faris Shohani's ordeal began in 1980. He was twelve years old. During the Iran–Iraq war his family was placed under surveillance and denounced as foreigners and spies. To be Kurdish Shia with ancestry in Iran was perceived as a threat by the paranoid regime of Saddam Hussein. Or was it simply an opportunity to seize possessions and homes?

Faris was at school that day. The police entered the classroom in the early afternoon. The teacher saw the colour drain from Faris's face. The headmaster, Mr Omran, protested, but the police ignored his pleas. Faris was escorted to the police station. His entire family was there: three brothers, four sisters, his mother and father, cousins, uncles and aunts.

They were interrogated for two days, stripped of their papers—birth certificates, passports, military service books, property deeds—and they were driven by army vehicles to the Iranian border with nothing but the clothes they wore. They were ordered to move on and not look back.

They crossed the border at night and lived for eight months in a refugee camp in a grass-floored tent, then in tents again for two years in a second camp. They were moved to a third camp where they lived for five years in a single room. Throughout their twenty-one years in Iran they were stateless. They had returned as strangers to the land their forebears had lived in a century ago.

Faris's great-grandfather was raised in the Zagros Mountains in Iran, near the border with Iraq. We have no friend but the mountains, so the Kurdish saying goes. But the mountains were unable to sustain them. Faris's great-grandfather had left the city of Ilam in search of a better life. He stole across the border into Iraq, made his way to the town of Badra, and finally settled in Wasit, now a two-hour drive southeast of Baghdad.

Faris shakes his head in wonder: 'When my family lived in Iraq, they said you are from Iran. You are not one of us. And when we were forced back to Iran, they said you are from Iraq, you are not one of us. The Kurdish people in the north of Iraq were Sunni and we were Shia. At school in Iran my children were called bad names. They were *Arabi* not Persian. We did not have passports. We did not have papers. We were not allowed to work.

'There was a kind man. He gave me a job in his factory. He was in danger for his kindness. I did not want him to have trouble. I did not want my children to suffer. We did not belong here. We did not belong anywhere. We were nothing.'

Aunty Joy guides me over Coranderrk Station. The people seized the opportunity, she says. They cleared the land, tilled the soil, dug irrigation channels, and planted wheat and hops. They built a school, a bake house, wooden houses, a brick homestead and a church. They ran cattle, produced cheese, butter and meat; set up craft industries. Market gardens. Turned a profit. Played by the rules of the new game.

Station manager John Green and his wife Mary sat with them, worked with them, raised their own children alongside the Kulin children. They learnt the Woiwurrung language, recognised the peoples' knowledge and love of Country, and their birthright to their lands. The Greens had come from the old world to the new, only to discover it was far more ancient than the old.

Again, the invaders fastened their eyes on the land. The people took a stand. With the death of Simon Wonga in 1875, Barak became the *Ngurungaeta* of the Wurundjeri. He was a man of many parts, says Aunty Joy—a spokesman, a diplomat and negotiator, a singer, dancer and craftsman, an artist who depicted Woiwurrung life. A keeper of knowledge. A leader of his people in dark times.

He had witnessed it all. He knew the stakes. He led three marches, sixty kilometres from Coranderrk to Parliament House, protesting plans to shut down the station. Barak and the people of Coranderrk filed petitions, wrote letters to newspapers, to the colonial government and to the Board that was set up to 'protect' them. They formed deputations, gave evidence at hearings and, after his dismissal as station manager in 1875, they fought for the reinstatement of John Green, the man who had sat with them on equal ground.

Big story this. Of men and women who battled to create a secure life for their children. Of underpaid wages and siphoned-off profits. Of a yearning for self-government and the formation of strategic alliances. Of rebels and resistors, broken promises and betrayals. The story is being reclaimed by the descendants. Hearing it told has deeply changed the way I see this land.

At first the resistors succeeded. Coranderrk survived, but it would not last. The odds were stacked against it from the start. It takes time for the true horror to sink in, the ruthless logic of dispossession, the greed. A body blow was dealt with the passing of state legislation in 1886: 'An Act to provide for the Protection and Management of the Aboriginal Natives of Victoria'.

Protection is a cruel euphemism. More accurate to call it by its popular name: the 'half-caste act'. It led to a policy of the forced removal of so-called 'mixed-race' residents under the age of thirty-five from missions and reserves. Sixty residents were ordered off Coranderrk, says Aunty Joy.

It was an act of violence. A violation. It ripped families apart, shredded communities, severed bonds of kinship and depleted the station of its labour force. It defined rights in accordance with self-serving hierarchies based on arbitrary classifications of race.

In 1893, the land allotted for Coranderrk was halved. Barak remained on the station till his death in 1903. When Joy's father, born and raised on Coranderrk, returned from the European battlefields, wounded after active service in World War I, he too was ordered off. He was deemed half-caste, says Joy, and judged to have no claim on the place of his birth.

The station was finally closed in 1924. Some of the remaining people were transferred hundreds of kilometres east to Lake Tyers. 'Why do you keep taking away things from us?' Aunty Joy quotes Barak. 'We are dying away by degree.'

There is a portrait of Barak, painted in 1899 by Victor de Pury, titled 'King Barak, Last of the Yarra Tribe'. The portrait is of its time. Idealised. Romantic. Enclosed in a gilt frame. It does not reflect his fierce resistance. Nevertheless, it is painted with a measure of respect.

The artist's father, Swiss immigrant and winemaker Guillaume de Pury, was a friend of Barak's. And Barak was a frequent guest in the De Pury home at Yeringberg, within walking distance of Coranderrk; it is said that the two men exchanged their knowledge of farming, that Barak explained the ways of his people and their deep kinship with their lands.

But there was a difference. Barak's movements, his place of residence and status were now subject to the dictates of the state. He was robbed of agency, not truly free to go where he wished. Barak could not meet his allies on equal ground.

Barak is painted with a mane of white hair and a full white beard. He wears a high-collared jacket. His gaze is distant, and intense. Says Aunty Joy: 'When I look at the King Barak portrait, I see my uncle as a proud and strong Indigenous Australian man. I also see the deep buried sadness of a heartbroken man.'

There is a Yiddish term, *luftmensch*. Literally 'person of air'. It describes a people who live on the margins and are forced to survive by their wits, subject to contested borders, restrictions in status and in fluctuating rights to the ownership of land.

It is a term that can apply to those torn from their places of birth. The refugee is a person of air. Uprooted, stealing across borders, scaling barbed-wire fences, languishing in camps. Seeking a way out. The refugee runs from one place to the next for so long, she no longer feels the ground beneath her feet.

Here, perhaps, is where we meet. The Wurundjeri were uprooted, and the land they had worked and sustained for millennia was taken by whatever means: the force of arms, guile and deception, and the rule of a foreign law.

In the portrait, the state of the *luftmensch* is intimated in Barak's gaze. It is fixed on a lost world, but it is also a world that lives on through him; and while he lives, the stories are being passed on to his heirs. His gaze is at once dignified and preoccupied. It breaks through time. It is a reminder: We are still here. We have not been broken.

That gaze. I know it well. I had seen it as a child in Meier and Hadassah. It could come upon them at any time, drawing them elsewhere. It was Hadassah's gaze as she moved about the house, singing Yiddish songs born out of the landscapes of her youth. She too was no longer tethered to the earth—raging: I have a story to tell. No one understands. No one sees. No one knows who I am.

She clung to her sense of self through song. Her mezzo-soprano voice reverberated in every room. Insistent, anguished at the edges, growing louder. Declaring: I am still here. You cannot take my voice from me. If you dare, I will raise it higher.

And it was the gaze I saw in my father when he returned from work. After the evening meal was done, he rose from the table with his eyes fixed on a distant point. It lured him through the dining room and the passage to the front bedroom, and to the dressing table, his makeshift desk. He sat behind closed doors, with his head bent over the works of Yiddish poets, writing of the landscapes of his youth.

He had brought the books with him from Poland. Flowers and leaves, gathered in the Russian–Polish borderlands, were pressed between the pages. He read the books many times over, and transcribed extracts and entire texts, and added poems of his own. I discovered the transcribed works just weeks ago. Written in notebooks, on strips of paper and pieces of cardboard, and assembled in a two-ringed folder between hard black covers. I had overlooked the folder when I'd gathered his writings and reflections in 1992, after his death.

There are 324 numbered pages. Some are reinforced by yellow tape. The Yiddish script of the poems is compact and neat, written in a calligrapher's hand. Meier's comments are scrawled in the margins. On the first page, in red biro, is a short prologue, titled 'A treasure'. Meier writes:

> Reflections, excerpts from works, entire texts of songs and poems from various authors, artists—people of great spirit, who have, in my journey through life, called out to me, requesting that I transcribe them, so that I can draw inspiration from them—a balsam for the soul.

As a child, I caught glimpses of Meier's world, places that would draw me on a quest to see them. Back then, I was more at home on the streets. Meier was a remote presence, up before dawn. I heard him pottering in the kitchen, making breakfast; heard the back door close and the back gate unlatch, as he set out via the back lane on the four-block walk to the Lygon Street tram. He was going through the daily motions, walking over bluestone lanes and bitumen paths on his way to work at the Victoria Market. His steps were light, the tread of a *luftmensch* making ends meet by selling socks and stockings.

But his mind was elsewhere. Only at the makeshift desk was he grounded. In transcribing the poems, he too was making a statement: No matter how far I have journeyed, I will keep you with me, my beloved poets, and the landscapes we once walked on. I have not abandoned you. You live on through me.

And I have seen that gaze, too, in Faris. It is haunted, and haunting: the gaze of a man stripped of his sense of belonging and defined as worthless. After twenty-one years of statelessness, Faris no longer felt the ground beneath his feet. It was time to get out. He was free of restraint. Weightless. Ready to take flight.

Faris's son, Ali, was nine, and his daughter, Zahra, seven, when the family sold all they possessed to purchase passports and tickets. They were flown to Kuala Lumpur and bused to Malaysia's east coast. They were in the hands of others: fishermen and smugglers, government officials, border police.

The adults waded out in the shallows with their children to a boat that took them to Sumatra. They travelled on by ferry to Java, where they lived for a time in a hostel with fellow asylum seekers en route to a new life.

Faris sought smugglers in Jakarta and in the markets of Cisarua. He was told to look out for the man driving a Mercedes. The man said he was only able to take four members of the family. He would accept payment once the boat arrived in Australia. He offered to take Ali for free. Ali left in mid-August with his grandmother, Fadilha, Faris's sister, Mina, and his brother, Mohamed. The boat made landfall at Ashmore Reef, 320 kilometres from the Australian mainland.

Faris continued his search. He was directed to the Egyptian smuggler Abu Quassey. At first, Faris was suspicious of his promises and his boasts of a spacious, well-equipped boat. Abu

Quassey charmed the children. They were drawn to his grand gestures and extravagant tales. A new Eden awaited them beyond the horizon, he told them. Just one last stretch of water, he assured him. You will see.

Zahra called him Uncle. Whenever Abu Quassey showed up at the hostel she would run to him, kiss him and say: 'Uncle, hurry up with our trip. I am missing Ali so much.'

Running short of money, Faris offered to pay in jewellery. When the deal was sealed, Zahra said, 'Uncle, thank you very much. Tomorrow I will see Ali.'

'Be like lions,' Quassey said. 'Don't fear anything. Leave the worry about Indonesian police to me. I will take care of everything.'

On 18 October 2001, Faris, his wife, Layla, and Zahra were bussed from a school building in Sumatra late at night. It was still dark when the 421 men, women and children were offloaded on a beach at the southern tip of the island. Waves lapped at their feet. The sea stretched out before them, an ominous presence. Smaller boats ferried them to a boat moored offshore. The women and children were taken out first; it was calculated they would offer less resistance.

As they neared the boat they were sickened by what they saw. Nineteen metres in length, four metres wide, the ageing fishing vessel bore no resemblance to the boat they had been promised. They could not imagine how it could brave the ocean. The women and children were transferred on board, and the men followed. The anchor was winched in. The boat moved out at dawn into unknown seas.

~

On the living-room bookshelf stands a model of a schooner, carved in wood. Faris bought it in 2008 after a journey to Indonesia seven years after the boat that became known as the SIEV-X—Suspected Illegal Entry Vessel number 10—sank. 'I did not want to return,' he says. 'I did not want to meet the ocean again. But my heart told me to go, and my mind wanted answers.'

He visited his old haunts. He returned to the hostel and the markets of Cisarua. He searched the ports for the fishermen who had saved him. 'I wanted to take them presents. I wanted to give them flowers. I wanted to give them cake. I wanted to say, you saved my life. I wanted to say thank you, you looked after me, but I could not find them. I ran here, I ran there. I asked many people. No one would help me. No one said anything. It was like a big secret.'

Faris returned home with nothing to show bar the model schooner. He lifts it from the shelf and shakes his head in wonder. He pauses, his eyes fixed on the intricate carving.

'The women and children were crowded on the lower and upper decks,' he says. He points at various places on the model. 'The men sat in the front, and on the cabin roof. They were here, over there, and on the roof of the engine house.'

Bodies leaned on bodies, heads rested on stomachs. People lay feet to feet, head to head, curved in foetal postures. Mothers held babies in their arms. Infants rolled into the bodies of sleeping strangers. People pushed for that extra centimetre of breathing space.

Faris sits back down on the sofa. He holds the schooner in one hand and places the other on his chest. 'I sat in the boat like this,' he says. He straightens his back, folds his hands in his lap, holds his body steady and stares at an unknown point. Then he sags back. With great effort, he lifts himself from the sofa and eases the boat back on the shelf. He returns to the sofa, folds his arms and straightens his back.

'Yes, I sat like this. I did not move. What did I care?' he says, maintaining a blank face. 'What did I have? What could I lose? I am suffering for what? I was hard. Nothing can shift me. To die was much better.'

Faris continued to sit in the same place on the boat even as, later that morning, twenty-four Mandaean Christians, fearing for their safety, disembarked near a group of islands south of the Sunda Strait. Many other passengers were tempted to join them. Faris had no desire to leave. He had rolled the dice, and that was that.

At night, the vessel rose and fell into deepening troughs. A collective prayer rose from the boat, a chant in a babel of languages: 'God, please save us. Please save us. God, help us.' Zahra clung to her father. Faris held her tight, and tried to shield her from the fury of the storm.

After many hours, the wind subsided. In the morning, the sea was calm. The children saw dolphins and leapt for joy. The captain announced they had passed the yellow buoy and were now in international waters, six hours from Christmas Island. Soon you will reach your destination, he said.

'Zahra, we are almost there,' said Faris.

Zahra clapped her hands. 'Are we going to see Ali soon?' she asked.

'Yes, God willing,' Faris replied.

In the early afternoon, the boat foundered. The engine was damaged. The captain called for any mechanics among the passengers to help fix it. The back-up machinery was old and corroded.

The sound of a plane lifted their spirits. The men dragged out T-shirts, jeans, blouses and shirts and set them alight. The smoke signals rose. The plane vanished.

The boat's engine stopped. The men laboured frantically to revive it. Men and women bailed the water with buckets and other containers. They could not keep up. The waters rose; the boat groaned and the planks cracked. To lighten the load, supplies and luggage were thrown overboard. Zahra wept as she saw the toys and batteries she had planned to give Ali disappear.

Still the waters rose. The boat listed. The panic spread. Then the men began to jump. Some leapt in silence, some with wild cries. Others stood by the edge, petrified. Faris held Zahra's hand on one side and Layla's on the other.

'Zahra, do not worry,' he said. 'We are together.' He braced his knees, hesitated. Wondered whether to chance it. The sea raged below them. Zahra pleaded for him to stay on board. 'We must be brave,' Faris said. 'I want to be with you,' Zahra replied.

A mountainous wave settled it. It happened quickly. The SIEV-X went down at 3.10 pm. People were screaming: 'God, help us. God, help us.' Some were trapped below deck. Others were flung into the ocean. Layla and Zahra clung to Faris.

Layla lost her grip. Zahra lost her grip. Faris saw Zahra slide into the ocean. He moved towards Layla. Layla screamed: 'Don't come to me. Go to Zahra.' Faris swam after Zahra. She was wearing a life jacket. He kept his eyes on her. She was elusive, bobbing in the water.

'I was like a fish,' Faris says. 'I swam quickly. I followed her, but she was faster. She was like melting butter.' She was beyond his outstretched hands, glimpsed in the troughs between waves. Appearing, disappearing. He searched and searched. He dived and resurfaced, drew on reserves he did not know existed. He swam until his body could no longer bear it.

Faris returned to Layla and found her floating, dead. There was no time to think. He was supported by a worn life jacket. He stands up to demonstrate. There were three pieces of foam: 'One here,' he says, pointing to his lower right back, 'and one there,' pointing to the left. 'And one under my head.' He tilts his head back to show me.

He is immersed in the telling. Debris floated by: suitcases, water bottles, oranges, apples, shoulder bags. Stuffed animals. Shoes. Thongs. Cooking pots. Pillows. Plastic toys. Pieces of timber. Slicks of petrol from the sunken boat. It was raining. Water beat down on water, clouds blurred the horizon.

At nightfall, the world sank into darkness. The rain ceased. An eerie silence settled on the ocean. The survivors had drifted apart. Faris floated alone. His throat burnt with saltwater. The waves swelled in a hypnotic rhythm. Then, approaching midnight, the boats appeared—two larger boats, and a smaller one.

'Three boats,' says Faris. 'I swear it.'

Their lights flickered out of the gloom. He paddled frantically towards them. He discovered there were many other survivors in the ocean. They clutched at debris in singles, pairs, in groups of six. They held on with one hand, and with the other they paddled. They screamed. They whistled. They shouted: 'Help. Please save us.' Searchlights probed the waters, illuminating the paddlers.

They were close, reaching out, almost touching. The hulls loomed like walls above them, then the boats backed away and withdrew into the darkness. 'They vanished. Just like that,' says Faris. He sits back on the sofa, returns his hands to his lap and resumes his motionless posture.

The desire to see Ali again kept him going. He held the image of his son before him. It was an antidote to his exhaustion. But when the boats abandoned him, he was finally broken. Faris leans back on the sofa. Again, he is elsewhere. Beyond the kitchen window the leaves are rustling.

Faris's gaze returns to the living room. He lifts himself from the sofa. He stands on the polished boards and continues his story: 'I did not care anymore. I lost all my feeling. I lay on my back. Like this.' He stretches full length on the floor. 'I rested my head on the life jacket.' He folds his arms over his chest, wriggles, and makes himself comfortable. 'The water was thick and salty. The jacket was my pillow, and my bed was the ocean. I closed my eyes and fell asleep.'

Faris awoke in the dark to rain and lightning. 'Where are the people? Where are the people? No one is answering. Everyone is gone. I am alone. I am with the ocean. I am with the wind. I am with the sky. I am with the water. I am with three bodies—a young boy, four or five years old, and a boy and girl, maybe eleven.

'Where did they come from? How did they find me? The bodies stuck to me. They did not leave my side. They were like children resting against their father.' Faris takes a deep breath. He unfolds his arms and places them behind his head. He lies back and gazes at the ceiling. 'This is how it was. I lay on the water. I did not care. I closed my eyes, and I returned to sleep. Just like that.'

I sit with Aunty Joy at her living-room table. I am overwhelmed by what she has told me. She knows the ebbs and flows. When Coranderrk was closed in 1924, five older people refused to be moved on, she tells me. They remained there until they died. In 1933, Joy's brother, James Wandin, was the last Aboriginal person born at the station, in the home of his grandmother, Jemima Wandin. Granny Jemima passed away in 1944. She was one of the last of the Wurundjeri to die at Coranderrk.

When Joy's father, James Henry Wandin, died in 1957, fourteen-year-old Joy tried to fulfil his final wish to be buried in the Coranderrk Cemetery, the last half-acre of Wurundjeri land. Her efforts were thwarted. Even in death, he was refused his birthright.

Yet the people endured. Family bonds were sustained, kinship remembered. In this we were determined, says Aunty Joy. The Wandin family and other Wurundjeri descendants continued living in Healesville and the Upper Yarra region. They retained their ties to the land, regardless of who now claimed title.

The resistance of the Wurundjeri never ended. Aunty Joy notes key dates. 1985 marked the creation of the Wurundjeri Tribe Land and Compensation Cultural Heritage Council. In September 1991, the Coranderrk Aboriginal Cemetery was handed back, the first half-acre regained. The following year the Wurundjeri acquired the ninety-four acres of the former army school of health. In 1999, another two hundred acres were returned.

The Wurundjeri are passing on lore, reclaiming language, marking the special places, the gathering sites on the banks of the creeks and rivers, and Mount William, the location of a stone axe quarry, once the epicentre of a vast trading system that extended seven hundred kilometres to the north. They are planting, rejuvenating areas of Coranderrk. They have never left, yet they are returning.

I drive northwest to Mount William and am guided over the greenstone quarries by Wurundjeri elders. I now know the maps. I drive around the bay, Boonwurrung territory, where the city hugs the coastline. I drive to Mordialloc and walk the banks of the creek to the sea entrance. I drive back northeast and break free of the suburbs into the Yarra Valley. Barak's country, now farmland and vineyards.

I cross the Great Divide via the Black Spur Drive and return hours later to Coranderrk Station. I have traversed this route many times now. In 2009, towns in the Acheron Valley were ravaged by bushfires. Many lives were lost, homes destroyed, properties wasted, swathes of forest reduced to charred trunks and bare black branches.

I crisscrossed the spur in the months after the fires to record the stories of survivors. I heard tales of fences melting like candle wax, of a woman trapped in a car between two walls of flame—the burning house visible in the rear-view mirror and the woodlands ablaze before her—thinking, it's so hot the windscreen is going to explode. She closed her eyes, put her foot on the accelerator, and drove through the flames to the other side.

I heard tales of the 1939 fires from one of the last living survivors, an ageing farmer. He was thirteen years old back then, working on his father's farm. 'Was so hot, all you had to do was spit to start a fire,' he says. He relives the sight of exploding eucalyptus, and of horses, their manes on fire, screaming as they tumbled down the hillside. His father lost his mates at the timber mills. 'Never saw him weep before. Never saw him weep since. Tell whoever is willing to listen that the fire will always come back. To live here, you must live with the knowledge of fire. No matter what you do, the fire will always come back.'

I have descended the Black Spur towards Acheron on many mornings and seen clouds lifting from the valley like plumes of white flames from obscured crevices. And I now drive homewards over the spur as darkness descends, after a day of bushfire stories. It rains. The road is treacherous. The forest leans in, branches swirl in the winds, the rain slants across the windscreen. I turn the wipers to high speed and grip the wheel as I take the sharp bends.

I am nervous, unsettled by the lights of oncoming traffic. If I slow down slightly, cars bank up behind me. I sense the drivers' damn impatience. They are crowding in on me, beeping their horns, raising their high beams, as if to say, 'Get out of the way, you idiot.' I seek out wider shoulders, pull over, allow them to pass, then return to the road.

My thoughts are under siege, possessed by what I am coming to know about this stretch of mountain. I think of a young man I had met that day: 'It went still, so still,' he told me, his voice falling to a whisper. 'And out of the stillness, arose a deathly roar, like a stampede of cattle coming over the mountain.'

He lost everything, his home, all he owned. He moved to a caravan park, and lived alongside others displaced by the fires. 'I now live for the moment,' he says. 'I am strangely free. I am light on my feet. Weightless.'

These stories too are now a part of me, interwoven with the tales of Wonga and Barak crossing the Great Divide, leading their people. They had no need to hasten, no need to career around hairpin corners. They knew the terrain. Knew that it could not be taken by force. Knew that they must walk it at a steady pace, guided by the contours, attuned to the land.

They knew how to work it, and how to conserve it; knew the texture of small things, what was edible, what was useful. They knew of plant communities now extinct and lost to memory, and they knew the power of fire and scorched earth, and the certainty of new growth. Knew the dangers and the beauty; the scent of it—their beloved Country, the solid ground beneath their feet.

Faris awakes to the rising sun. The three bodies are still by his side, as if reassured by his presence. In the distance, he makes out a fishing boat. He cannot believe what he sees. He no longer trusts his own vision. His limbs ache. He is hungry and thirsty. Salt clings to his tongue. It sours his mouth and sears his lips.

He sees a black plastic bag floating by. He paddles over and grabs it. Inside there are three red apples, two packets of biscuits, and a bottle of water. He starts with the water, and drinks all of it. He eats the three apples; the biscuits he keeps for later. He now has energy for another twenty-four hours. The water and the apples have given him hope.

A seagull settles on his head. It is very light. In the distance, Faris sees two fishing boats; and he sees a whale, swimming towards him. He is scared. He says to himself: 'Faris, you are gone now.' He says: 'I did not drown, but this will finish me.' He prays. The whale dives and disappears below him.

Faris paddles towards the fishing boat. As he draws close, the three bodies leave him. 'I never mentioned this before,' he tells me years later. 'What happened was amazing. As soon as I came near the boat the three bodies went one way, and I went the other. I watched them float away. I said to them, "Thank you. I will never forget you. You did not leave me. You kept watch over me. You stayed with me through the night."

'The fishermen threw down a rope. I reached up and grabbed it, and they pulled me out of the water. I was the first one saved. They lifted me onto the deck. They helped me up. They hugged me. They were very kind. They led me to a shower. They gave me tea, and they gave me food and water. They were sitting beside me. They put their arms around me. I showed them a photo of my wife and daughter. I told them, I want to go to Christmas Island.

'I said, "Please take me."

'They said, "We can't."

'The captain said, "We are going back to Jakarta."

'I said, "No, you must look for other people."

'The fishermen told me they saw only dead bodies and luggage. I told them, "There are fifty people out there." The fishermen had good boats. Strong, timber boats and a satellite. The captain was a good man. He said, "Okay, we will look."'

Faris saw each survivor rescued. He was lowered on a tyre to haul in some of them. They were lifted on board in shock, exhausted, weeping. They collapsed on deck. For a moment, they were frantic with relief, but relief soon gave way to panic.

Their cries rang out: 'Where is my son? Where is my daughter? Where is my wife? Where is my mother? My father? My aunt, my uncle? Where are my brothers and sisters? Please you must look. You must save them!' They sank to their knees, tore at their hair and their damp clothes, and beat their fists against their foreheads and shoulders. They fell at the captain's feet, and wrapped their arms around his legs. Faris is still haunted by their pleas.

'Why?' he asks. 'Why?' His voice falls to an urgent whisper. 'Why did the boats leave us? Why?' It is years since the sinking and the question still plagues him, as it plagues the forty-five survivors dispersed over many lands—Sweden, Norway, Canada, New Zealand and Finland—including the seven who settled in Australia.

In the early years Faris would ring survivors living in other countries. They talked for hours. They talked through the night united by a common fate, churning over the details of the event. Why this, and what if that? They clung to each other's voices, staving off the return to the desolation they felt when the calls ended.

He no longer calls. 'I am tired. They are tired. I have no answers; they have no answers. What can I say to them? It is the first question they ask: "Why, Faris, why? Why did Abu Quassey put us on that boat? He knew it wasn't safe. He knew the weather was no good. He knew the engine was old. He knew the boat was dangerous."

'Why did the boats leave us? Why?' I saw the boats. They saw the boats—two bigger boats, and one smaller boat. But they left us, and still we don't know why. This question makes us sick.'

I am back on the Black Spur Drive, mid-winter 2019. There is something about driving on treacherous roads flanked by dark forests that leads me to speculate. What does it mean to have one's story ignored or denied? What does it mean to be hounded and left homeless? What does it mean to belong? To feel at home, grounded?

Meier and Hadassah never travelled over the Black Spur. They had no need or the desire. They were done with journeys. As they entered their seventies, they finally acquired the house they had rented for decades. The landlord had died. He lived in New Zealand. Never once did he visit or get in touch. He left all supervision to the real-estate agent. The house was put up for auction in 1970. The prices in our gentrifying suburb were about to soar, putting houses out of reach of families who had lived in them for generations.

On the day of the auction we gathered outside our home: my two brothers, long-time neighbours, friends and supporters. And Hadassah and Meier, fearful of what lay ahead. They could not imagine living anywhere else. They could not contemplate another move, beginning anew in another location. One more uprooting would have been unbearable, perhaps fatal.

There remained a sole bidder against them. He had appeared at the last minute and positioned himself in front of the crowd. He was a calm, calculating rival, dressed in a suit, white shirt and tie, casually lifting his finger as the bids mounted. He looked straight ahead, impassive. We reached our limit. Our rival countered. We made one last desperate bid. He shrugged his shoulders, returned to his car and departed.

A cheer went up. The onlookers had been drawn into the drama. They recognised the stakes. We drank a toast on the median strip, under the palms and poplars—that stretch of paradise my father loved to look at from the front window when he lifted his head from the works of the Yiddish poets.

The change in my parents' sense of wellbeing was instant. They had secured their tiny space on earth. They walked with firmer steps to the corner stores, the milk bars, and to and from the nearby shopping centre. They rejoiced in the familiar. They knew every shopkeeper—the newsagent, the barber, the shoe repairer, the baker and chemist, the butcher, the greengrocer, the delicatessen, the fruiterer and the hardware manager. They engaged with them in conversation. Big talk. Small talk. It did not matter.

They lived out their lives in that house and the neighbourhood, grounded by its solid presence and nourished by its certainty. It was all they wanted, and all they needed. Meier made his way daily to Curtain Square and his bench beneath the Moreton Bays. He inhaled the scent of figs fermenting on the path, and breathed easy. Then he returned on that one-block walk from Curtain Square to Fenwick Street, and a hundred metres further, to his single-fronted terrace house, the proud owner.

In her final years, Hadassah retreated into the depths of the house. She slept in the back room. It was her fortress, shielding her from the ghosts that continued to besiege her. On warm days, she sat on a chair in the backyard, enclosed by tin and paling fences, the secure borders of her private domain. Hands folded on her lap, eyes closed, allowing the sun to bathe her.

She moved about her tiny kingdom, shoulders rounded, from the yard to the washhouse, and along the brick path to the kitchen door. She sat for hours at the table, as the sunlight withdrew from the window, along with the stove, the refrigerator, the fireplace, the enamel sink, the shelved alcove, and the plywood cupboards—her anchors. She sat as darkness descended. Her voice rose from and returned to silence, and with it the song: *How still it has become, the night has come to stay. The white beryosé remains; standing in the forest alone.*

By the time they died, Hadassah in 1990, Meier in 1992, they had lived in the house far longer than they had in any other place. Upwards of forty-five years. More than half their lives.

~

Faris and Majida too have no desire to be elsewhere. This is where they wish to live out their days. They too take comfort in the familiar: the stairs to the wire-mesh door, which opens directly into the kitchen. The tree outside the window. Their bedroom; their living room.

'He cannot be away for long,' says Majida. 'Only here, he feels safe. When he visits his mother, Fadilha, and his son, Ali, he cannot stay still. Within half an hour of arrival, he is nervous. "Majida, we must go back," he says. "Why?" his mother asks. "You have just come." "No, I must go," he says. He is panicking. He must return home to our flat.'

'Would you risk the sea journey again?' I ask. 'Of course!' Faris replies. 'For years I was no one. My brain became hard. My heart was tougher than rock. Nothing could frighten me. Nothing could hurt me. Too much they pushed me in Iran and Iraq. Too much they said I was dirt. We have a saying: "If someone is wet, he is not afraid of the rain."'

'This is my home now,' Faris tells me with a wave of his hand. 'This is my palace. Everything.' He gestures to the window: 'This is my country now. I love it. I want to look after it. I do not like to see rubbish on the streets. I cannot understand why people throw rubbish in such a beautiful place. I pick it up and put it in the bin.

'Thank God. Iran and Iraq are finished for me now. Finished.' He flicks his hand in a dismissive gesture. He glances downwards, and taps the floor with his foot. 'This is my earth now.'

And there is the lullaby Faris sings in his sleep. Majida recites the lyrics in Arabic and translates: *Don't cry, your mum is coming back soon. She's bringing you toys, a bag full of toys. One of the toys is a duck, and it goes quack, quack, quack.*

Faris lights up at the memory. 'Zahra learnt this song from an Egyptian man who lived with us when we waited for the boat in the hostel. His name was Ibrahim. He had a daughter, Sara. She was four. She played with my daughter.

'The Egyptian man told Zahra, "I will teach you a song." Zahra sang the lullaby to me. She tickled my stomach whenever she said "quack, quack, quack".' Faris laughs. Then the light drains from his face. 'Ibrahim and Sara were on the boat with us. When the boat sank, they vanished.'

He leans forward and buries his face in his hands. Hidden somewhere in the flat are the shirt and trousers he wore in the ocean, stiff with salt. He cannot throw them out. All that remains of Zahra is a doll and a handbag. Zahra had left them behind in Indonesia. They too are hidden in the flat. Faris retrieved them in Jakarta after the fishing boats returned from the rescue. He has kept them close by ever since. I am haunted by the doll and the handbag, though I have never seen them. I dare not ask.

Yet, there are saving graces, forces that keep Faris going. There is his son, Ali. He still lives with his grandmother, Fadilha. Faris sees him often. And there is Majida. Her journey mirrors his. She tells it only when I ask.

Majida's Kurdish forebears too made the journey from Iran to Iraq in search of work. Majida was fourteen when, in 1982, Saddam's police came for her family in Baghdad. They were ordered out of their home at night and detained in a hall with more than one hundred people. In the morning, they were taken on buses to the Iranian border and abandoned. They slept where they were dumped, and set out at first light.

They walked through the day and the night. They rested the next day and continued in the evening. Late at night, they came across a patrol of Iranian soldiers. They had left two of Majida's brothers imprisoned in Baghdad. Her father did not care about the loss of his home and possessions, and his truck-hire business: everything he had worked for. He was worried only for the two sons.

It was after the fall of Saddam Hussein, in 2005, that he learnt of their fate. They had been killed in jail in 1990, two among the thousands of Kurdish men tortured and murdered, or used as human minesweepers in the warring borderlands. When he heard the news, Majida's father had a heart attack. He died a year later, a broken man.

Accompanied by a brother and two sisters, Majida had left for Indonesia in 2000. They boarded a boat in Sumatra for the final leg of the journey. On the third day at sea they sighted a plane with a kangaroo insignia and were elated. The boat made it to Darwin and the sisters spent four months in the Port Hedland Detention Centre. After their release, they settled in Sydney.

'Sometimes I love October, and sometimes I hate October,' says Majida. 'I arrived in Australia in October, but my mother died on a day in October. My family was deported from Iraq in October, and the boat that took Zahra and Layla's lives sank in October. I knew about the people who drowned on SIEV-X, and

I knew about Faris before I met him.

'When he came to see me in Sydney he told me everything. He told me he was always sick and worried. He showed me his medication. He told me he could not sleep at night, and he told me that sometimes he did not want to talk to anyone. I told him, no worries. I want to be with you. I could see he was a kind and honest man. I told him, "Faris, I will move with you to Melbourne." I told him, "Faris, I will marry you."'

Now, after many visits to Faris and Majida's flat, I can see it. Now that we have sat together, side by side by the living-room coffee table, in talk and in silence, I am beginning to understand it: this story of immense loss. It will always be that. The stain will never be washed off.

But there is something else. It is in Majida's stoic demeanour, in the tone of her voice, and in her ease, the measured way in which she moves from the kitchen to the living room, bringing food and drink to the table.

It is in the way she moves about the flat, mindful of Faris's presence; and in her complete absence of judgment, the way she allows Faris's stories to rise from and return to silence; it is in her attentiveness no matter how many times he tells them. And it can be heard as she sings Zahra's lullaby. This, too, is a tale of love.

I am a child of people of air. Hadassah and Meier's journeys saved their lives but, for years to come, imprisoned them with the ghosts of their loved ones. I am the beneficiary, free to travel of my own will and free to choose my destinations. I can take flight.

The plane lifts me above and beyond the city. It arcs over the bay and veers back inland. It carries me across the Great Divide, a vast stretch of plateaus and mountain ranges. For 3700 kilometres, the Great Divide follows the eastern coastline. It is a watershed, host to rivers flowing east to the coast, and west, inland. It can be seen from the plane window where the land breaks free of the gridlines of city streets and highways, fenced farmlands and homesteads into the vastness of untamed terrain.

I am flying to the interior, the red centre, and north into the Territory, and then out west to the Kimberley—from the forested ridges of the Great Divide to white inland saltpans, from secluded bays to red dirt and jagged escarpments. I have a birds-eye view of the continent—river tributaries and estuaries fanning out like leaf veins. Creeks twisting between ridges, carving gullies. Looking down on swirls of pale blues and violet, ochres and purples, broken by arrow-straight roads shooting towards receding skylines.

I have begun to walk land that has been walked, and worked, for millennia. Begun to know a tiny fragment of the living quilt of Indigenous Country. I have walked in the wake of rains beside once-dry riverbeds now raging waterways. I have circumnavigated rock monoliths glowing at dusk like red phantoms; have walked where long-dormant seeds have burst briefly into flower. And I have begun to walk with some of those who possess stories for each rock, each stream, each constellation and waterhole.

A big story this. And an old story: where there is dispossession, there will be resistance. This is how it is. 'It's going to rain,' the old man says. 'Give it six hours, but believe me it's going to rain. Best place to be is here, sitting in the shade beneath the house.'

Several times a year, I take the now-familiar route by way of the Yarra Valley, left at the Woori Yallock turn-off and, several hundred metres on, right into Barak Lane. I pull up at the Coranderrk Cemetery, unchain the gate and fasten it behind me. The cemetery stands on a rise, enclosed by wire fences. I have been coming here for a quarter of a century now, since the day that Aunty Joy first guided me.

It is autumn. The ground is strewn with decaying leaves and toadstools. Mounds of discarded bark wreathe the bases of eucalypts. Alpacas wander down to drink from the dam. A black bull moves by, lowing. Crows forage in the paddocks. The winds are rising, all is movement: branches and saplings, clumps of grasses and wild daisies.

Among the graves there is a headstone for Winnie Narrandjeri Quagliotti, Wurundjeri elder, a leader in the fight for recognition. When Winnie died, in August 1988, she became the first Wurundjeri buried in the cemetery in more than four decades. Nearby is a granite memorial stone dedicated to William Barak.

Further on, there is a moss-encrusted cairn with steel plaques, recording the story of the trek across the Black Spur and the history of Coranderrk Station. And the names of the people who found their final resting place here: beginning in 1863, the year the people returned.

There are many Wurundjeri names, Kulin names, and names belonging to other tribes from throughout the state now known as Victoria. Babies and infants, teenagers, adults, long-lived elders, marked alone or grouped in families, their dates of birth and death recorded. Below them are engraved the words of poet Oodgeroo Noonuccal: 'We belong here, we are of the old ways.'

It is well over a century since William Barak's passing. There is a photo of him seated on the veranda of his wooden cottage beside his dog in his final years on Coranderrk. I imagine him from this half-acre, my gaze fastened on vast expanses of sky and the surrounding ranges.

Like his great-grandniece, Aunty Joy, Barak was open, willing to receive visitors who came in good faith, proud to demonstrate the ways of his people and to pass on stories and language, vocabularies of Woiwurrung that would become one of the sources for the reclamation of language by his descendants. His dignity cut through, and his presence drew people to him. His being transcended his enclosure, and undermined the prejudices of those who saw him as a curiosity.

The sun, a globe in the west, is hitting the peaks, sending shafts of light over the valley. I imagine Barak speaking of his homelands. He speaks, as people who knew him have described it, in a slow, gentle voice. He sweeps his hand over the ranges.

He resisted all attempts to move him. He belonged to the creeks and the rivers, to the Birrarung, and to the volcanic plain that defines the river's course and beyond, to pathways and trading routes that are woven into the fabric of an entire continent. And always, at the heart of it, to the mountains of the Great Divide, and his place overlooking the valley. Aunty Joy quotes his words years later: 'Yarra, my father's country.' He would not be moved. He would never leave it.

And in years to come, my mother and father would find their tiny space within it: Hadassah and Meier, the song and the poem, in their single-fronted terrace; and Faris and Majida, in their one-bedroom apartment, the resting place for a lullaby. Hadassah and Meier, Faris and Majida: they came from the old world to the new and found refuge in a world far more ancient than the old.

Meier and Hadassah are a part of this earth, buried now in Kulin country. And Majida and Faris are a living part of it. They walk each afternoon in Princes Park. On clear days, to the east, in the far distance, can be seen the ranges of the Great Divide; and to the south, the city's core, a huddle of office towers and high-rise apartments; and, closer, the sandstone facades of university colleges.

Majida and Faris sit on a park bench as evening falls. There is space, acres of grass, oaks and elms, palms and eucalypts. Children play in the small playground fifty metres away; their mothers keep a watchful eye. Faris hears the chirping of birds and the voices of children. For a blessed moment, he is fully present.

And yet...Faris sags back in his seat. He feels hot. His haunted expression returns. His gaze turns inward. He names them. Zahra. Layla. Ibrahim. Sara. Four among 353 men, women and children—all gone, their resting places unmarked, forever en route, in the ocean. And the boats abandoned them: 'Why? I will never understand it. Why? Why?'

~

A station wagon pulls up to the bitumen space in front of the cemetery. A young man steps out, unlatches the gate, and makes his way to the cairn. He pauses in front of the plaque and searches. His eyes linger on one name. He runs a finger over it. He steps back and stands for a long while head bowed, then makes his way to the fence. He sits, legs folded, and looks out over the valley.

And I know. I know without having to ask. He has located the name of an ancestor; and I know he is feeling something of what I felt in 1986, in cemeteries on the outskirts of the towns whose names I first heard sung in that distant kitchen. *Bransk, Bialystok, Grodek, Orly, Bielsk.* Seeking family names among untended gravestones dispersed over fields, hidden in woodlands, sinking into abandoned plots obscured by wild grasses. And of what I felt in Treblinka, where I lit a candle at the stone marked Bialystok and retreated to a forest of conifers to sit on a floor of raw dirt and pine needles.

We sit within the same half-acre. We sit as the evening closes in. We sit as the mists begin descending, and as the mountains fade to black skylines enfolding rolling farmlands. A flock of migrating birds wings overhead in V-formation. A chorus of frogs rises from the dam. The shrill cry of cicadas rings out in the valley. We sit as the land gives way to nightfall. Here is where we meet.

Author's note

The title story of this collection, 'The Watermill', is set in a period that can be viewed as an interregnum between the Cultural Revolution, which ended in 1976, and the 1989 Tiananmen Square massacre. I lived and travelled widely in China in 1984–85 and was based in Guizhou Province for much of that time. I thank my colleagues and students at the Guizhou Agricultural College, and other people I met in China, for the journeys and stories they shared with me.

I have combined a range of separate incidents and encounters to create composite stories and composite characters, and I have used letters for names and monikers to protect the identities of the people whose tales I have drawn on. I have also changed some specific details as an added precaution.

Revisiting my time in China, I was struck anew by the Tang and Song dynasty poets. The poems of Li Bai, Du Fu, Wang Wei, Han Shan and others ring true many centuries after they were written. The title story is influenced by this poetic legacy.

In 'The Ballad of Keo Narom', I have again disguised the identity of individuals by creating pseudonyms and composite characters, except for Keo Narom and Voy Ho. My conversations with Narom initially emerged from the mutual recognition of the impact that genocides had on our families. The person I call 'R' organised the writing workshops in Phnom Penh, Siem Reap and Battambang between 2013 and 2015. He interpreted my talks at the workshops and my conversations with Keo Narom. I thank him for his knowledge, the journeys we shared, and his deep concern for Cambodia and its people. 'The Ballad of Keo Narom' was also informed by R's memories of the Khmer Rouge era as a child. Without him, this story could not have been written.

I thank Phina So, writer and advocate for Khmer literature, for her constructive reading of the story and for enhancing my understanding of contemporary Cambodia. Oum Sophany, a participant in the workshops, wrote and spoke eloquently of her experiences of the Pol Pot era. She died in June 2018. I thank the Cambodian writers who attended workshops, some of whom invited me into their homes and accompanied me on some of my journeys.

I am indebted to Joan Healy for her careful reading of the manuscript. Joan has devoted years of service to Cambodia and its people. The verse on page 114 of the song 'And You Plough' is my translation of Chaim Zhitlowsky's original Yiddish.

Sami Feder's memoirs, which I read in the original Yiddish, provide the foundation for 'Republic of the Stateless'. They include: *Gebaylte foystn,* Clenched Fists, Tel Aviv, 1974; *Durkh tsvelf gehenem-fayern,* Through Twelve Fires of Hell, Tel Aviv, 1985; and *Mayn Lebn,* My Life, Tel Aviv, 1995. I also drew on

Feder's *Notes on a Diary of the Yiddish Studio 'Kazet Theatre' in Bergen-Belsen 1945–1947.*

I delivered a tribute to Sonia Lizaron at her memorial service, a version of which was published in the journal *Meanjin* in December 2016. As I researched the story further, hearing from Arie Olewski and Jochevet (Jochi) Olewski was indeed a pivotal moment, and I am greatly indebted to them for our conversations, for information they sent me and their enthusiasm for the project.

I also draw on the work of researchers Sophie Fetthauer—whose essay 'The Kazet-Theatre and the Development of Yiddish Theatre in the DP Camp Bergen-Belsen', appears in *Dislocated Memories: Jews, Music, and Post-war German Culture,* edited by Tina Fruhauf and Lily E. Hirsch—and Zlata Zaretsky, who met Sami Feder in his final years. And I thank Brazilian-based researcher Leslie Marko for our many discussions about the Kazet Theatre. Marko's recently published doctoral thesis on Sami Feder and the Kazet Theatre is titled: *Teatro De Sami Feder: Espaço Poético de Resistência nos Tempos do Holocausto (1933–1950).*

I am indebted to Elly Trepman for checking passages of the story for historical veracity. As the years go by, and with the rise of Holocaust denialism, the need to be faithful to history grows more urgent. Hence I have drawn on many primary sources to check the historical facts.

Elly's mother, Babey Trepman, was a pianist in the Kazet Theatre. His father, Paul Trepman, helped Sami Feder edit the *Zamlung fun Kazet un Ghetto Lieder*: Anthology of Songs and

Poems from the Ghettos and Concentration Camps, 1945; and Babey wrote the music. Paul also acted as a spokesperson alongside Sami Feder on the theatre's tour of Belgium and France.

Elly Trepman's article 'Rescue of the Remnants: The British Emergency Medical Relief Operation in Belsen Camp 1945', an account of the British-led relief effort after the liberation of Bergen-Belsen—which draws on testimonies of British troops, doctors, relief workers and camp residents, and on articles published in the *British Medical Journal* and *Lancet* in the late 1940s—provided useful information.

I made use of the following books: Ben Shepherd's *After Daybreak: The Liberation of Bergen-Belsen, 1945*; Angelika Konigseder and Juliane Wetzel, *Waiting for Hope: Jewish Displaced Persons in Post-World War II Germany*; and *Jewish Displaced Persons in Camp Bergen-Belsen, 1945 and 1950: The Unique Photo Album of Zippy Orlin*, edited by Erik Somers and Rene Kok. I also drew on eyewitness accounts published by the Imperial War Museum, London.

'Republic of the Stateless' is not a history of the Bergen-Belsen displaced persons camp and its complex politics, which included the ongoing conflict between the Jewish residents and the British authorities over restrictions to immigration in British-controlled Palestine. My story focuses on, and was inspired by, the life of Sonia Lizaron, born Sonia Boszkowska. Sonia was a dear friend for more than thirty years. I was also informed by many conversations over the years with Bono and Pinche Wiener and Abram Goldberg.

The songs of Shmerke Kaczerginski and Mordechai Gebirtig

are deeply imbedded in Yiddish culture. I grew up hearing and singing them. Kaczerginski's 'Springtime' has been translated into English many times. I have drawn on a range of translations in constructing my own. Other song and poetry credits include: Hirsh Glick, 'Quiet the Night' and 'Never Say'; Mordechai Gebirtig, 'It's Burning'; Itkhak Manger, 'Solitary'; Sami Feder, 'The Shadow'; H. Leivik, 'Eternal'; and Moshe Shulstein, 'A Mountain of Shoes'. Sonia Lizaron's album *In Joy and Sorrow* was recorded in Tel Aviv in 1966.The term 'republic of the stateless' is figurative. Officially, the inmates were designated 'displaced persons', a term that was widely used during and immediately after World War II for people who were removed from their native countries as refugees, prisoners or slave labourers.

For the record: The Jewish Central Committee of Bergen-Belsen Displaced Persons Camp was formed on 18 April 1945. The Cultural Department of the Committee, according to Sami Feder, was co-founded by himself, Sonia Boszkowska, Josef Rosensaft and Dr Hermann 'Zwi' Asaria-Helfgott, with Feder as artistic director. At its peak, the Kazet Theatre had thirty members, whose individual deeds have been documented and honoured in Sami Feder's memoirs.

The final story, 'Where We Meet', was set in motion by my conversations with Wurundjeri elder, Aunty Joy Murphy Wandin, which I first wrote of in the feature article, 'A Tale of Two Cities', published in the *Age*, Melbourne, September 1995. The bigger story was seeded when I was invited to contribute to *The Intervention: An Anthology*, edited by Rosie Scott and Anita Heiss. The book brought together Indigenous and non-Indigenous authors writing in a range of genres. 'Where We Meet,' is a greatly expanded version, and in some ways, a quite different story, interweaving a major new strand—the tale of refugee and SIEV-X survivor Faris Shohani.

I am indebted to Aunty Joy Murphy Wandin, for sharing her knowledge and experience of her people's history and for guiding me to the special places. I thank Jim Berg, founder of the Koori Heritage Trust, for the workshop he conducted and for introducing me to Aunty Joy. I thank Wurundjeri elders Uncle Bill Nicholson Snr, Margaret Gardiner and Annette Xyberras and Boonwurrung elder Caroline Briggs for showing me significant sites back in the mid 1990s.

The story of Coranderrk has received much attention in recent years. It features in the Verbatim Theatre play, *Coranderrk: We Will Show the Country*, based on the testimonies, minutes and proceedings of the 1881 Parliamentary Inquiry into Coranderrk and first performed at La Mama Theatre in 2011. The book by the same name, by Giordano Nanni and Andrea James, 2013, includes a detailed history of the Station. In 'Where we Meet', however, I have largely confined the story to my journeys with Aunty Joy Murphy Wandin back in the 1990s.

I met Faris Shohani in 2002, soon after his arrival in Melbourne from Indonesia. I thank Faris and his wife, Majida, for their kindness and hospitality over the years, and their courage in telling their stories.

I am grateful to the survivors who took part in the 'Black Saturday: Telling the Stories' project in 2009 and 2010. The book, *Ten Years On,* by Melanie Harris-Brady, one of the participants in the project, personifies the courage and the ordeal endured by the survivors.

I thank Michael McGirr and Rod Moss for reading the manuscript and providing positive feedback. Other generous readers included Adrian Hyland, Frank de la Rambelya, Christine McKenzie and Tina Giannoukos.

This is my seventh book with Text, and my fourth book with Jane Pearson as editor. I am grateful for her great skill, insight and support. Jane seeded the idea of interweaving the threads that form the final story.

This book has been assisted by the Australian Government through the Australia Council, its arts funding and advisory body.

Hadassah and Meier, my parents: you were both, in your different ways, heroic.

As always, I thank my partner, Dora, and son, Alexander. Your support makes it possible.